PAUL GIAMATTI HOPE DAVIS

AMERICAN SPLENDOR

ORDINARY LIFE IS PRETTY COMPLEX STUFF

Screenplay by
Robert Pulcini
and
Shari Springer Berman

with an Introduction by the authors

Carhil Ventures, LLC

American Splendor: The Official Shooting Script

Copyright © 2003 by Home Box Office, Inc. All rights reserved. ® Home Box Office, Inc.

Library of Congress CIP data available from the publisher.

ISBN 1-56649-952-6

Photos by
JOHN CLIFFORD

Printed in the United States by
HAMILTON PRINTING COMPANY

Interior design by
MULBERRY TREE PRESS, INC.
(www.mulberrytreepress.com)

First edition: September 2003

3 5 7 9 10 8 6 4 2

CONTENTS

For Nanny Rose, our favorite "Old Jewish Lady."
You'll always be in our hearts . . .

INTRODUCTION

by Robert Pulcini and Shari Springer Berman

NEARLY EVERY SCREENWRITING BOOK AND FILM CLASS teaches one cardinal rule: a movie should be rooted in the most dramatic situation possible. Be it a western, a love story, or a horror film, the conflict at the heart of the story must be heightened and extreme. Yet what immediately drew us to the *American Splendor* comic book series was the way Harvey Pekar chronicled the mundane, sometimes poetic, yet always honest moments of everyday life—the kind of stuff most people would edit out of their memories, let alone a movie. While this admittedly made *American Splendor* a daunting subject to take on, in our eyes Harvey was a true pioneer whose life's work was worthy of a movie. Long before the development of the consumer video camera or the explosion of so-called "reality" TV, this Cleveland file clerk/jazz critic/obsessive collector chronicled decades of his unremarkable existence in a medium that was once *reserved* for the remarkable: comic books. And as filmmakers with a foundation in documentaries, we strongly connected with his impulse to tell real stories about real people.

So how exactly do you begin adapting a comic that prides itself on untidy narratives? Our first step was to look at the nearly three decades' worth of comic books (and the *Our Cancer Year* graphic novel) as one long, epic work rather than a series of disjointed, individual issues. By approaching the material in this macro way, a whole life comes into focus—one with a classic dramatic structure of love, loss, loneliness, creative longing, and life-and-death struggles. We then read (and read and read) the comics until we discovered an overriding theme for the material: ultimately, this was an unconventional love story between a man and his art form. We then selected stories and incidents from the comics that inform this narrative line—the tale of a seeming loser who puts together a life through art. The fact that his art happens to be comics and that he is more of an "inaction hero" than an "action hero" is what made *American Splendor* unique and exciting.

Now that we had a general storyline, we faced another big obstacle—how to incorporate the real Harvey Pekar into his own biopic. Despite logistical issues, we believed Harvey's indelible persona would grant authenticity and texture to the film. Our solution came from the fact that so many different artists draw Harvey in his comic books. We felt this gave us the license to play with different incarnations of Pekar: the "movie Harvey" to be portrayed by Paul Giamatti; the "animated and comic-panel Harvey" to be drawn by artists from R. Crumb to Doug Allen; the "real Harvey of the present" to be played by Pekar himself; and "the real Harvey of the past" represented in actual footage from his infamous appearances on *Late Night with David Letterman*.

Because the film's resulting structure is a bit unorthodox, we are often asked how *American Splendor* was initially designed in screenplay form. Therefore, the version we decided to publish here is our "shooting script"—the one that existed during the actual filming. No doubt you will find inconsistencies with the way the movie eventually unfolded, as our writing process continued well into the editing room (where we had the luxury to toy with text boxes and other comic-book elements). In addition, this shooting script includes several imagined documentary sequences. While one can never bank on how the unpredictable Mr. Pekar will react to a line of questioning, we wanted this screenplay to fully reflect our hybrid vision, so we took a stab at guessing. Ultimately we were fully prepared to throw these "place-holder" documentary sequences in the garbage. Obviously the final documentary sequences that appear in the film were not scripted, but to this day we're still amused by how far off or how close we actually came.

Writing the screenplay was one thing, but we could have never pulled this movie off without our amazing team. So many wonderful, dedicated people supported our vision and devoted themselves to making *American Splendor* into a movie. There are simply too many names to list. They know who they are and we thank them all for joining us on this unforgettable journey. Our first day of casting was on the eve of September 11, 2001, at the downtown Manhattan offices of the now-defunct Good Machine. Our opening weekend was on the eve of the largest blackout in North American history—affecting three of the four cities where we opened (and purported to have originated outside of Cleveland!). As Harvey says, "Ordinary life is pretty complex stuff."

—Robert Pulcini and Shari Springer Berman

American Splendor

Screenplay by

Robert Pulcini
and
Shari Springer Berman

FADE IN:

INT. HARVEY'S BEDROOM - NIGHT

A BEDROOM MIRROR.

The room is dark. A perfectly square mirror hangs crooked on
a wall.

Suddenly, out of the darkness, the reflection of a man's face
comes into focus. He stares straight ahead, perhaps studying
his own unrecognizable reflection. It's quite clear this is a
portrait of sickness; the man's pallor is gray, his eyes are
confused. There is something most definitely wrong.

Tentatively, the figure steps away from the mirror, leaving
the frame empty and dark.

ANGLE ON BED

Like a ghost, the naked man (HARVEY) stands over his bed
staring down at his sleeping wife (JOYCE). In the eerie
light, he's almost translucent.

                    HARVEY
                 (faintly)
         Joyce ... Joyce?

Joyce springs up, alarmed.

                    JOYCE
         What's wrong, Harvey? What are you
         doing up?

Harvey just stands there for a moment saying nothing.

                    JOYCE (CONT'D)
         What is it?

                    HARVEY
                 (delirious, out of breath)
         Tell me the truth. Am I some guy who
         writes about himself in a comic book?
         Or am I just --am I just a character
         in that book?

Joyce rubs her eyes.

                                        (CONTINUED)

                         JOYCE
          Harvey ...

                         HARVEY
          If I die, will 'dat character keep
          goin'? Or will he just fade away ...

Joyce just stares at him, unsure how to answer. Suddenly
Harvey collapses.

Joyce leaps from the bed, nervous, hysterical. She gets down
on the floor and shakes him.

                         JOYCE
          Omigod Harvey! Harvey, wake up!

CLOSE ON HARVEY'S FACE

His eyes remain closed, his expression far, far away.

                                              FADE TO BLACK:

EXT. CLEVELAND ROW HOUSE - FALL - 1956 - DUSK

FADE UP ON:

A surreal kaleidoscope of black, white and red. Similar to
the mirror scene above, the colors slowly come into focus,
revealing the chiseled features of a familiar face. But this
time we see that it is not a real face, but rather a plastic
mask of the D.C. Comic hero -- SUPERMAN.

INTERTITLE: CLEVELAND OHIO, 1956

CLOSE ON SUPERMAN MASK

It glows eerily in the light of a porch lamp. A child's
pupils glare through the eye holes ...

The camera pans from SUPERMAN to the masked face of another
caped-crusader: BATMAN. Batman turns towards his loyal side-
kick ROBIN, who clutches a plastic, trick-or-treat pumpkin.
Next, we find THE GREEN LANTERN as he reaches up to ring the
doorbell. The camera finally rests on the last boy: an
unkempt KID wearing no costume at all.

Looking irritated and removed from the rest of the group, the
KID shoves his hands in the pockets of his shearling coat. He
spits and rolls his eyes as a lady answers the door.

                                              (CONTINUED)

The brick home is as working class as it gets. The lady at
the door is a 1950's HOUSEWIFE.

                    BOYS
               (in unison)
          Trick or treat!!

                    HOUSEWIFE
          Well, look at this! All the super-
          heroes on our porch! Ain't that cute.

The Lady drops a candy apple in each boy's container.

                    HOUSEWIFE (CONT'D)
               (still yelling)
          We got Superman here, Batman, his
          sidekick ROBIN, ohh, The Green Lantern
          even ...

She finally stops at the costumeless KID. He halfheartedly
holds up a ratty, stained pillowcase.

                    HOUSEWIFE (CONT'D)
          And what about you young man?

                    KID
          What about what?

The other boys giggle. The kid flashes them a "kick yer ass"
look.

                    HOUSEWIFE
          Who are you supposed to be?

The kid shrugs.

                    KID
          I'm Harvey Pekar (pronounced "Pee
          Car").

                    HOUSEWIFE
          Harvey Pekar? That doesn't sound like
          a super hero to me...

                    BOYS
               (mumbling)
          Pecker, Pecker ...

                                              (CONTINUED)

                              KID
            I ain't no super hero, lady. I'm just
            a kid from the neighborhood, alright?

The Housewife stares at him, confused.

                              KID (CONT'D)
            Ahh, forget this...

Frustrated, the kid throws his pillowcase down. He trudges
off as the others watch in confusion.

                              KID (CONT'D)
            Why is everybody so stoopid?

BEGIN NERVOUS JAZZ SCORE

WE FOLLOW the schlumpy kid (aka HARVEY PEKAR) as he sulks
down the street...

                                             DISSOLVE TO:

EXT. CLEVELAND ROW HOUSE - FALL - 1975 - DUSK

INTERTITLE: CLEVELAND OHIO, 1975

A grown-up version of HARVEY PEKAR (now mid-thirties) stomps
along the same Cleveland street. Unfortunately, 20 years
have made this rust belt neighborhood a bit rustier. The
"GROWN UP HARVEY" dons the same shearling coat, sports the
same disheveled hair, and wears the same curmudgeonly
expression.

CREDIT SEQUENCE - ANIMATED SEQUENCE

INTERCUT HARVEY WALKING WITH COMIC BOOK PANELS OF THE CARTOON
HARVEY IN ACTION. This is not your typical super-hero stuff.
Instead it features our man engaging in such daredevil feats
as:

INT. CITY BUS - FALL 1975 - DAY

--Riding the city bus.

INT. V.A. HOSPITAL - DAY

--Working as a file clerk at the Veteran's Hospital.

INT. HARVEY'S APARTMENT / KITCHEN - DAY

--Trying to wash dishes.

INT. SUPERMARKET - DAY

--Waiting on line at the supermarket.

EXT. GARAGE SALE - DAY

--Buying used records from a garage sale table.

INT. GREASY SPOON DINER - DAY

--Eating junk food at a greasy spoon.

INT. HARVEY'S APARTMENT - DAY

Harvey fixes a rip in his coat with Elmer's Glue.

(Note: Each "Cartoon Harvey" looks similar but unique... a
variation on a theme. This is because his cartoons are drawn
by different comic artists.)

Intermittently, bold cartoon credits flash across the screen:

FROM OFF THE STREETS OF CLEVELAND COMES ...

Followed by the explosive title:

AMERICAN SPLENDOR

The high-energy music and upbeat titles -- in direct contrast
to the sulking image of Harvey -- continue through the
remainder of the credits.

EXT. CLEVELAND STREET OVERLOOKING FACTORIES - DAY

We're now on HARVEY'S back as he continues his forlorn journey. We move forward, past him, to peer over the hill at the
factories below.

                    REAL HARVEY (V.O.)
               Okay. We're throwin' a lot at ya
               here, so lemme step in an' help ya
               catch up. This is a story about comic
               books, an' a guy who made a whole
               life outta them. You could even say
                         (MORE)

                                              (CONTINUED)

                          REAL HARVEY (V.O.)(CONT'D)
                    comics saved his life. This guy
                    here, he's our man, Harvey Pekar --
                    all grown up and goin' nowhere.
                    Although he's a pretty scholarly cat,
                    he never got much of a formal educa-
                    tion. For the most part, he's lived
                    in shit neighborhoods, held shit jobs,
                    and is now knee deep into a second
                    disastrous marriage. So if yer the
                    kinda person who's lookin' for romance
                    or escapism or some fantasy figure to
                    save the day, guess what? Ya got the
                    wrong movie.

SUDDENLY EVERYTHING--THE MUSIC, THE CREDITS, THE IMAGES--
COMES TO A HALT.

                                                        CUT TO:

INT. SOUND STAGE - PRESENT - DAY

HIGH DEFINITION VIDEO DOCUMENTARY FOOTAGE

The REAL HARVEY PEKAR (not the actor who trudged through the
credits) sits behind a microphone, supplying the "voice over"
above. He clutches a movie script in his hand.

The frame is spare, with a few well-chosen items to indicate
that he's in a recording session.

Although he is significantly older than the man who portrays
him, the "Real Harvey" is every bit as much of a sad sack...
maybe even more.

He is large and slightly threatening with knitted brows and
wild eyes. Yet there is something kind and vulnerable about
him -- a teddy bear who could kick your ass.

Off Camera, WE HEAR the voices of the male and female direc-
tors (us -- BOB and SHARI) coaching the "Real Harvey" through
his voice over. Harvey's irritable and contrary, saying that
the whole Halloween incident never even happened. "But I
don't care man. I'm just doing this for the dough." We learn
that Harvey is a reluctant participant in a film being made
about his life.

                                                        (CONTINUED)

SUDDENLY, his third wife JOYCE BRABNER -- an intelligent con-
trol freak obsessed with all things negative -- joins in the
conversation. Pushing back her huge glasses, she reprimands
Harvey like he is an infant: "Harvey you are talking too
loud, Harvey you are being difficult." Harvey just rolls his
eyes. Joyce gets offended. It is clear they have had this
argument a million times. As Joyce storms off...

Harvey explains that his wife is trying to take over the
movie. He laments that she is his third wife, and he has no
luck with women. "Man, chicks just don't dig me." That's
why he marries anyone who will have him. "And I marry them
fast before they get to know the real me..."

END HIGH DEFINITION VIDEO DOCUMENTARY FOOTAGE

CUT TO:

INT. EXAMINATION ROOM - WINTER - 1975 - DAY

INTERTITLE: 1975

HARVEY sits on a table in his T-shirt and underwear. A DOCTOR
unwraps a tongue depressor.

Harvey's voice is hoarse, raspy and barely audible. It sounds
like it hurts for him to talk. Yet, he can't stop ranting.

> HARVEY
> Doc, you gotta help me. My old lady's
> dumping me 'cause I can't talk. She
> says I'm a social embarrassment. Now
> that she's got her PhD, she's some
> hot shit academic star an' I'm
> nuthin' but a file clerk with nothin'
> ta say an' no voice ta say it. But me
> bein' a file clerk was fine when I
> wrote the damn check for her tuition--

> DOCTOR #1
> Harvey, stop talking please, and open
> wide.

He points the tongue depressor at Harvey's mouth but he just
keeps on going.

                         HARVEY
          I just don't get it ... We were doin'
          okay for a while. Then we took that
          stupid belated honeymoon. I started
          losin' my voice on the plane. Can you
          believe that... On the plane, doc?

                         DOCTOR #1
          Bad timing, I guess. Now please say
          "Ah," Mr. Pekar.

                         HARVEY
          "Ahhh."
                    (without missing a beat)
          "Ahhh" ruined the trip. I got crazy,
          started to worry my voice would never
          come back.   I mean, my wife didn't
          know me so long before we got
          hitched. What if she totally forgets
          what I'm like? Man, it's torture--

                         DOCTOR #1
          Shhh ....

The Doctor shines a penlight into Harvey's mouth and looks
around.

                         DOCTOR #1 (CONT'D)
          Uh-huh.

He raises an eyebrow. Harvey catches this. Hypochondria over-
takes him.

                         HARVEY
                    (the penlight in his mouth)
          What? Is it bad, doc?

The Doctor removes the penlight.

                         DOCTOR #1
          It's not good.

Harvey jumps off the table.

                         HARVEY
          It's cancer? First I get marital prob-
          lems and now yer tellin' me I got
          throat cancer? Omigod ...

                         DOCTOR #1
              Harvey, calm down. It's not cancer. You
              have a nodule on your vocal chords.
              Probably from screaming and yelling
              too much. And if you don't stop talk-
              ing and give it a rest, you're gonna
              lose your voice completely.

Relieved, Harvey calms down. He nods, agreeing to be good.

                         HARVEY
              Whew ... Okay, okay. But fer how
              long?

                         DOCTOR #1
              A few months.

                         HARVEY
                    (loudly)
              Months!!

Suddenly Harvey's voice cracks under his effort to raise it.
He sheepishly grabs his throat.

                         DOCTOR #1
              See? More of that and you'll do per-
              manent damage. Now go home, keep
              your mouth shut, and hopefully we
              won't have to operate.

Operate? Harvey gets nervous again. The Doctor throws him his
clothing.

                                                      CUT TO:

EXT. CLEVELAND STREET - WINTER - 1975 - DAY

A silent sequence. A dejected HARVEY walks home alone along
an empty lot. Day-old dirty snow clings to the ground.

He wanders through a down-in-the-heels neighborhood, passing
run-down stores and ramshackle apartments.

EXT. BUS STOP - WINTER - 1975 - DAY

Harvey approaches TOBY -- a dumpy 20-something going on 60-
something in ridiculous, mismatched polyester clothing. He is
odd, awkward and talks with a monotone, robotic voice. In
short, he is a super dork.

                                                  (CONTINUED)

> TOBY
> Hi Harvey. You weren't in work today.
> Are you okay, Harvey?

Harvey barely looks up. He nods his head "yes" and keeps walking.

> TOBY (CONT'D)
> (yelling after him)
> I'm heading downtown to the White
> Castle. Wanna come, Harvey?

Harvey leaves Toby behind and turns the corner.

EXT. DELI - WINTER - 1975 - DAY

Two WOMEN argue loudly over a payphone.

> SPANISH WOMAN #1 (IN SPANISH)
> *I already told you, I'm waiting for a*
> *call!*

> SPANISH WOMAN #2
> *Oh yeah? Since when is this your*
> *private office!?*

> SPANISH WOMAN #1
> Since you can kiss my ass.

Harvey stops in his tracks and stares at them, jealous of their ability to speak.

CLOSE UP: SPANISH WOMAN #1's MOUTH

> HARVEY
> (to himself)
> Look at 'em yakkin'. How do they do
> it?

Out of the corner of her eye, WOMAN #2 notices Harvey eaves-dropping.

> WOMAN #2
> (yelling at Harvey)
> Ay, what you looking at? *Maricone!*

Startled, Harvey moves on.

EXT. ACROSS FROM A PARK - WINTER - 1975 — DAY

He passes a group of KIDS playing in the snow. They scream,
yell and laugh with abandon.

                    HARVEY
               (shaking his head)
          They all make it seem so easy.

Then, BAM! Harvey is awakened from his reverie by a snowball.
The kids laugh loudly. He wipes away the snow and walks on.

A VOICE OVER interrupts the scene.

                    REAL HARVEY (V.O.)
          Here's our man walking home from the
          doctor's. He's got the weight of the
          world on him. And fer what, really?
          'Cause his throat's a little screwy?
          Man, people in India are starvin' to
          death every day. His problems are
          nothin'.

                                        CUT TO:

EXT. BRIDGE OVER TRAIN TRACKS - DAY

Totally dejected, HARVEY crosses over train tracks on his way
home.

                    REAL HARVEY (V.O.)
          Still, he can't help feelin' paranoid,
          like some supernatural force is con-
          spiring against him to rob him of his
          voice.

EXT. HARVEY'S APARTMENT - WINTER - 1975 - DAY

Harvey sulks up the steps of his brick low-rise apartment
building. He passes an ELDERLY NEIGHBOR coming down the walk
with her shopping cart. Harvey unlocks the door.

                    REAL HARVEY (V.O.)
          Maybe his old lady will go easy on
          him today, when she sees how upset he
          is.

                                        CUT TO:

INT. HARVEY'S LIVING ROOM   - WINTER - 1975 - DAY

Harvey's second wife LANA -- a hippyish chic with long hair
and a bad attitude -- pulls books off a shelf and selectively
throws them onto the floor or packs them into a milk crate.
An overstuffed suitcase sits beside her. She's obviously
leaving him. HARVEY enters the room.

> HARVEY
> (whispering)
> Ay ... What is this?

Harvey's voice breaks up.

> LANA
> Exactly what it looks like.

> HARVEY
> (loud)
> Whattya mean!! You mean yer dumpin'
> me?! Fer what?
> (his voice really rips)
> Ah, shit!

That last yell did it. Harvey grabs throat in pain, torn
between his throat discomfort and trying to stop his wife
from leaving.

> LANA
> Look, your plebeian lifestyle isn't
> working for me anymore. Cleveland's
> not working for me anymore. I gotta
> get out of here before I kill myself.

> HARVEY
> But--

She gathers her bags and heads for the door. Harvey trails
her, trying to reason.

He opens his mouth, but nothing comes out.

> HARVEY (CONT'D)
> (mouthing, just a wheeze)
> Please! Wait, honey ... Just listen
> to what I got to say ...

She turns and stares at him. Harvey tries to say something. But
now nothing at all comes out of his mouth. Only wheezy air.

(CONTINUED)

He tries again. No sound at all.

Finally LANA gives up, turns back towards the door and
leaves.

SLAM!!

                                                        CUT TO:

INT. V.A. HOSPITAL - 1975 - DAY

At his cubicle in the file room, Harvey fills a cart with
files. He's physically at work, but mentally in a daze.

                    REAL HARVEY (V.O.)
              Here's our man--yeah alright, here's
              me --or the guy playin' me, anyway,
              though he don't look nothin' like me,
              but whatever. So it's a few months
              later an' I'm workin' my flunky, file-
              clerk gig at the V.A. hospital. My
              voice still ain't back yet. Things
              seem like they can't get any worse...

A nurse pops her head in. Harvey hands her a file.

                    NURSE
              Thank you, Harvey dear.

He doesn't hear her, still stewing about LANA. He shoves the
last files in the cart and pushes it away.

                    HARVEY
                   (to himself)
              Plebeian ... where the hell did she
              get that shit?

                                                        CUT TO:

INT. FILE ROOM -- A FEW MOMENTS LATER

We see rows and rows of endless files ...

Still in a daze, Harvey removes the files from his cart and
puts them on the shelves.

                                                        (CONTINUED)

                              MR. BOATS (O.S.)
                    Avoid the reeking herd!
                    Shun the polluted flock!
                    Live like that stoic bird,
                    The eagle of the rock!

Harvey turns around. Mr. Boats -- a portly, African-American
maintenance worker wearing a bow-tie -- steps into Harvey's
row. He has a tool box.

                              HARVEY
                    Huh? Oh. Hiya, Mr. Boats.

Harvey resumes shelving.

                              BOATS
                    You know what that means, son?

                              HARVEY
                    Yeah. It's from an Elinor Hoyt Wylie
                    poem. It means stay away from the
                    crowds of common ordinary people an'
                    do yer own thing.

Mr. Boats laughs.

                              BOATS
                    Nope, it means don't compromise your-
                    self for women. Ain't gonna do you no
                    good! Get away from 'em as soon as
                    you can!

                              HARVEY
                    Well I ain't got no woman now. So
                    I'm living like the stoic bird, man.

                              MR. BOATS
                    The only way to live, son.

Somehow this doesn't make Harvey feel any better about his life.

INT. HOSPITAL HALLWAY -- DAY

Harvey carries an armful of files. Mr. Boats still trails
him, lugging his tool box.

Suddenly, Mr. Boats points out a young African-American FILE
CLERK wearing a pair of headphones on his afro. He moves
as if he's listening to music.

                                                        (CONTINUED)

> MR. BOATS
> Look at that fool over there. What's
> he wearing?

> HARVEY
> Huh? That's an A.M.-F.M. radio he's
> listening to... They got 'em fixed up
> now like a pair of earmuffs.

> MR. BOATS
> (INAPPROPRIATELY ANGERED)
> MMPH! Isn't that somethin! People
> have gone crazy. They'll buy any
> kinda junk! Probably listening to
> that loud rock stuff. Junk, junk,
> it's all junk!

> HARVEY
> Well, I don't know. Rock music's got
> some good qualities. I mean it ain't
> jazz or nothin'.

Mr. Boats looks at him like he's crazy.

> MR. BOATS
> Say, when you gonna bring me in some
> good records? Some Nat "King" Cole
> with Strings...

> HARVEY
> I don't got any of that, Mr. Boats...

Mr. Boats stops and yells down the hall at Harvey.

> MR. BOATS
> Yeah, you got it... You're keepin' it
> at home, though! You won't turn
> loose the good stuff... You just sell
> the junk!

Harvey shakes his head as Mr. Boats finishes his diatribe.
Mr. Boats turns into a room.

> MR. BOATS (CONT'D)
> (singing)
> *Mona Lisa, Mona Lisa. Men have named*
> *you.*

                                                        CUT TO:

INT. SOUND STAGE - PRESENT - DAY

HIGH DEFINITION VIDEO DOCUMENTARY FOOTAGE

Harvey sits on outdoor furniture. A few props are featured in the frame indicating a garage-sale-like setting (including a record player). Directly in front of Harvey are boxes of used records.

HARVEY shows us his prodigious record collection. Thousands of LP's -- rare jazz, blues, fusion, klezmer, etc. -- are piled in floor-to-ceiling bookcases.

He tells us about his love of jazz and how he started writing jazz reviews and music articles. He finds the first record that he reviewed and puts it on his turntable. As the music plays...

Harvey talks about how he started buying and selling records. This leads into how he first met ROBERT CRUMB.

                                        DISSOLVE TO:

EXT . CLEVELAND GARAGE SALE - FALL - 1962 - DAY

INTERTITLE: 1962

HARVEY (a little more hair but the exact same style) and a bunch of his BUDDIES sift through old records at a junk sale.

                    REAL HARVEY (V.O.)
          In the early sixties I was with some
          buddies at a junk sale looking for
          some choice sides when I met this
          shy, retiring cat from Philadelphia
          named Bob Crumb. You know the guy;
          Fritz The Cat, Mr. Natural an' all--
          they made a movie about him, too.

One of Harvey's pals -- MARTY -- pulls a record out of a box.

                    MARTY
          C'mon, Harv. You dig Jay McShann. You
          gonna buy that or what?

Harvey jumps up from his search to check out the LP.

                                        (CONTINUED)

>   HARVEY
>   I don't know, Marty. It's got a lami-
>   nation crack in it...
>   (checking out the price)
>   A quarter. Maybe I can get him down.

>   MARTY
>   You are one cheap bastard Harvey.

>   HARVEY
>   Yeah, I know I'm tight, man, but I
>   live on a government wage.

A skinny guy with a big nose, glasses and a ratty trench coat
taps Harvey on the shoulder. He is soft-spoken, a bit shy and
very odd -- a young ROBERT CRUMB.

>   CRUMB
>   You collect Jay McShann, man?

>   HARVEY
>   Yeah, man. How 'bout you?

>   CRUMB
>   Yeah but most of my records are back
>   in Philly.

A greaser-type guy in a leather jacket, PAHLS, joins them.

>   PAHLS
>   Harv, meet my buddy Bob Crumb. He
>   just moved to town. He's an artist
>   at American Greeting Card Company.

>   HARVEY
>   That's cool.

>   PAHLS
>   You should see his comics, Harv.
>   They are outta sight.

>   HARVEY
>   (interested)
>   Yeah? I'm into comics myself.

>   DISSOLVE TO:

INT. HARVEY'S LIVING ROOM - FALL - 1962 - DAY

A disheveled mess that gives new meaning to the term bachelor pad. Records and book are strewn everywhere.

> REAL HARVEY (V.O.)
> So Crumb showed me this comic book
> novel he was working on -- THE BIG
> YUM YUM BOOK. I'd never seen anything
> like it.

HARVEY marches back and forth holding Crumb's illustrated comic novel. CRUMB sits on the floor nursing a beer and sorting through vintage comic books. Harvey's bursting with so much enthusiasm, it's almost aggressive.

> HARVEY
> It's terrific, man! I really dig your
> work.

Crumb ignores Harvey's praise.

> CRUMB
> (holding up a vintage comic)
> This PETER WHEAT book is by Walt
> Kelly... It's pretty rare.

> HARVEY
> Yeah? Can I get good bread for it?

> CRUMB
> Nah! Not yet.

Harvey flops down in an overstuffed chair. Stuffing flies out. He sips his beer.

> HARVEY
> Listen man, let's get back to your
> book. What are you gonna do with it?

> CRUMB
> (looking up)
> I hadn't thought about it. It's just
> an exercise.

Harvey flips through the book.

(CONTINUED)

                    HARVEY
          It's more than an exercise. It's
          breaking ground, man. There's some
          wild shit in here.

Crumb is immune to Harvey's enthusiasm.

                    CRUMB
          You're spitting on me, Harvey.

                                        CUT TO:

INT. HARVEY'S LIVING ROOM - FALL - 1962 - LATER

CRUMB lies on the couch sketching while HARVEY reads more of
THE YUM YUM BOOK. A scratchy jazz record plays.

                    REAL HARVEY (V.O.)
          Crumb and I hung out a lot back then.
          We had records and comics in common.

ANGLE ON CRUMB'S DRAWING

We see Crumb is actually sketching Harvey, slumped in a chair
reading a book. Crumb makes Harvey look like a smelly, sweaty
madman with ratty clothing.

Crumb holds the sketch of Harvey up to show him.

                    CRUMB
                  (laughing)
          Check it out, man. Pretty scary.

Harvey glances up at his portrait, completely unself-
conscious.

                    HARVEY
          Yeah, ya don't know the half of it.

Harvey goes back to reading. Crumb back to sketching.

                    REAL HARVEY (V.O.)
          Eventually people got hip to Crumb's
          art work and he started hangin' out
          with a Bohemian crowd. After a while,
          he got sick of greeting cards and
          moved away to San Francisco where he
          got the whole underground comic scene
          off the ground.

                                        (CONTINUED)

Crumb slowly evaporates from the room, leaving Harvey totally alone.

ANGLE ON 45 RECORD SPINNING AND SPINNING

>   REAL HARVEY (V.O.) (CONT'D)
>   He'd come back ta Cleveland every few
>   years, an' people'd treat him like a
>   celebrity.

The record spins and spins ...

END FLASHBACK

>   DISSOLVE TO:

EXT. BUS STOP - 1975 - DAY

ANOTHER R. CRUMB DRAWING OF HARVEY (Now circa 1975)

On a sketch pad we see a deranged, tormented Harvey sitting alone on a park bench. He pulls at his hair, and looks as though he may murder the next person who walks by.

INTERTITLE: BACK TO 1975

As the pencil adds shading to Harvey's face, WE HEAR:

>   REAL HARVEY (V.O.)
>   Once he came to visit when I was
>   really feelin' bad. It was right
>   around the time of my throat opera-
>   tion, an' right after my second wife
>   left me. At first it was pretty
>   weird. I mean, here my life was
>   falling apart an' everything was going
>   great for him. I was on my second
>   divorce an' he was a big hit with the
>   chicks. I was a nothin' file clerk
>   and he was this famous cartoonist.

HARVEY and R. CRUMB sit on a park bench together by a bus stop. A distraught Harvey whines while Crumb just sketches. Harvey's voice is still raspy.

>   HARVEY
>   I dunno, man. On the one hand most
>   women gettin' graduate degrees wouldn't
>   (MORE)

>   (CONTINUED)

>   HARVEY (CONT'D)
>   give a guy like me the time a' day.
>   An' she married me an' everything, so
>   I gotta give her some kinda
>   credit. But then she got so mean to
>   me in the end. An' it ain't like I
>   tried t'keep her captive or anything
>   like that, y'know?

Crumb may or may not be listening to Harvey. It's hard to
tell.

>   HARVEY (CONT'D)
>   An' then on top of it I lost my voice
>   for three months. I still sound like
>   shit, but before I had nothin'. Man,
>   talk about hell. I started forgettin'
>   what I sound like, y'know? So I
>   started writin' stuff down--stories
>   an' things, my points a' view, ideas.
>   I even published a couple jazz record
>   reviews. I guess that ended up bein'
>   a good thing.

>   CRUMB
>   Uh-huh.

>   HARVEY
>   But don't think I buy into this
>   "growth" crap. Everybody talks about
>   how bad experiences can cause ya
>   t'grow, an' all that clichéd stuff.
>   I've had enough bad experiences and
>   growth to last me plenty.
>   (a beat)
>   Right now, I'd be glad to trade some
>   growth for happiness.

For a moment, they both just sit there saying nothing to each
other, each man in his own private universe.

Finally Harvey looks over to Crumb.

>   HARVEY (CONT'D)
>   So how long are ya stayin' in
>   Cleveland?

Crumb never looks up from his picture.

>   (CONTINUED)

                              CRUMB
            I dunno, man. I gotta go visit this
            chick in New York. And I'm really
            busy with the comic book stuff. It's
            good bread and all man but I'm get-
            ting fed up with the whole scene.

                              HARVEY
            What are ya talkin' about? Yer makin'
            a good living doin' yer art? Sheesh.
            How many guys get that lucky in their
            life, huh?

                              CRUMB
            Yeah, I dunno.

                              HARVEY
            Ya know man, people are startin' to
            know the name "Crumb." When you croak,
            you're gonna leave something behind.

                              CRUMB
            Yeah, my ashes and some crappy doo-
            dles. It's not like I'm Blind Lemon
            Jefferson or Big Mama Thornton.

                              HARVEY
            C'mon, man. It sure beats workin' a
            gig like mine -- being a nobody
            flunky and sellin' records on the
            side for a buck.

                              CRUMB
            Yeah, well that's true ...

Harvey nods in agreement, mulling this over. He's not at all
offended.

                                              CUT TO:

INT. V.A. HOSPITAL - 1975 - DAY

CLOSE ON A FILE DRAWER MARKED: "RECENTLY DECEASED."

A hand reaches into the frame and opens the drawer.

By rote, HARVEY fumbles with a large stack of "expired
patient" files. He places each into the appropriate alphabet-
ical "deceased" drawer.

                                              (CONTINUED)

Attempting to grab another batch, Harvey accidently knocks
the entire pile onto the floor.

                    HARVEY
          Damn it!

He crouches down to survey the mess -- a collage of "expired
lives" laid out before his eyes.

We move past dozens of anonymous names -- William Anderson,
Louis Collins, Mark D'Amico, Tyrone Moore, Franklin Ray,
etc... Each file has a red "Deceased" stamp.

Depressed, HARVEY is transfixed by the files surrounding him
on the floor. Suddenly he stops and picks one up.

ANGLE ON FOLDER: It is marked, "CHARLIE MARSHALL."

He opens the folder and reads the stats...

Born: 1920 in Cleveland
Died: 1967 in Cleveland
Occupation: Clerk

ANGLE ON HARVEY: He swallows hard as he reads about
Charlie's small, invisible and now vanished life...

He tosses the folder back onto the pile.

                                        CUT TO:

INT. HARVEY'S APARTMENT - 1975 - MORNING

CLOSE ON: TWO STICK FIGURES IN AN EMPTY FRAME

HARVEY sits at a table with a pen in hand and a blank sheet
of paper in front of him. Nothing seems to come to him.

He flips through a pile of comic books -- everything from
D.C. Comic Super Heroes to underground works such as Crumb's
Mr. Natural and Zap Comix. No inspiration. Harvey throws them
down in frustration.

                    HARVEY
          I'm starvin'.

                                        CUT TO:

INT. SUPERMARKET - 1975 - DAY

HARVEY pushes a cart through the cramped aisles of a crowded supermarket. He pulls a few cans of Beef-A-Roni off the shelf and heads off to pay. Reaching the check-out area, he evaluates the situation.

ANGLE ON CHECK-OUT COUNTERS:

There are three lines to choose from. Two of the counters have long waits. The third is much shorter but there is an OLD JEWISH LADY next in line.

SUDDENLY, THE SCREEN SPLITS IN TWO:

The LEFT SIDE OF THE FRAME remains Harvey at the supermarket deliberating over the check-out lines.

However, the RIGHT SIDE OF THE FRAME now contains a CRUMB STYLE COMIC PANEL DEPICTING THE EXACT SAME SCENARIO. A BUBBLE appears over CARTOON HARVEY'S head revealing his thoughts. It reads: *"Pickin' the right check-out line is an art...There's a lot of things you gotta consider."*

ON THE LEFT HAND SIDE OF THE FRAME... Harvey decides to get behind the Old Lady.

MEANWHILE ON THE RIGHT HAND SIDE OF THE FRAME... Cartoon Harvey stands behind the Old Lady.

A new BUBBLE reads: *"It may be the shortest line but I am takin' a chance 'cause she's an Old Jewish Lady."*

BACK TO THE LEFT SIDE OF THE FRAME... The CASHIER rings up the Old Lady's purchases -- a few kitchen glasses.

> OLD JEWISH LADY
> (Yiddish Accent)
> Listen, goily, dese glasses are six
> for $2.00 because I couldn't carry
> twelf... But I vanted twelf so today
> I'm buying six more... But you should
> only charge me $1.50 for dem... It's
> ok, you can esk de meneger.

Harvey rolls his eyes and stamps his foot impatiently. He knows he's in trouble now.

(CONTINUED)

                        CASHIER
                       (yelling)
            Frank! I need a price check.

SUDDENLY, THE RIGHT SIDE OF THE SCREEN BECOMES FULLY ANI-
MATED... Instead of still comic panels with balloons, the
Cartoon Harvey now rants directly into the camera.

                    CARTOON HARVEY
            Man, Old Jewish Ladies will argue
            forever with a cashier about anything.
            Get behind them in a line an' yer
            gonna wait forever!

The Human Harvey seems oblivious to his cartoon replica.
He impatiently leans on his cart, waiting and seething.

                 CARTOON HARVEY (CONT'D)
            I mean, I'm a yid myself, an' the
            women in my family are like that...
            But I never got used to it... I may
            be cheap, but I got limits!

ON THE LEFT HAND SIDE OF THE SCREEN... The MANAGER finally
arrives. The Old Lady haggles with him, too.

                    OLD JEWISH LADY
            Please. Let me 'splain von more time.

MEANWHILE ON THE RIGHT HAND SIDE... The Cartoon Harvey turns to
address the Human Harvey, who actually looks him in the eyes. It
now seems Human Harvey can actually hear his cartoon alter ego.

                    CARTOON HARVEY
            Wake up! You're whole life's gettin'
            eaten away by this kinda crap! What
            kind of existence is this? Is this
            all a workin' stiff like you can
            expect? Ya gonna suffer in silence
            fer the rest a' yer life?! Or ya
            gonna make a mark. Huh? Huh?

IN AN INSTANT, THE CARTOON HARVEY DISAPPEARS AND THE LIVE
ACTION SCENE TAKES OVER THE WHOLE FRAME.

Suddenly motivated by an odd notion, Harvey abandons his gro-
cery cart and runs out of the supermarket.

                                              CUT TO:

INT. HARVEY'S KITCHEN -- NIGHT

Bursting with ideas, Harvey (wearing his undershirt and boxers) starts story-boarding his first comic with stick figures.

DISSOLVE TO:

INT. HARVEY'S KITCHEN - 1975 - MORNING

A bleary-eyed HARVEY, still clad in an undershirt and boxers, dozes off over a bowl of Corn Flakes. On the table next to some spilled milk are a stack of papers covered with scrib- bling. He clearly has been slaving over this work all night.

ANGLE ON PAPERS:

At the top is a quickly scribbled title, "Standing Behind Old Jewish Ladies In Supermarket Lines."

These are ad hoc versions of a comic book. The pages are divided like a tick-tack-toe board. Each square is filled with crude stick figure drawings and lots of writing.

An alarm clock goes off. Harvey's eyes fly open.

                    HARVEY
          Shit. Work.

Harvey yawns, then notices the pile of papers. He peruses them, proud of his work. He gets up and looks out the win- dow.

I/E. HARVEY'S APARTMENT - HARVEY'S POV - 1975 - MORNING

It is yet another grey day in Cleveland. The neighborhood is run-down. Garbage is strewn everywhere.

The following scene unfolds through the window:

Two UNSIGHTLY WORKERS lug an old, smelly mattress from a garage towards the garbage cans on the curb. Their conversa- tion is distant, but entirely audible.

                    MATTRESS GUY #1
          So how smart is she?

                    MATTRESS GUY #2
          I dunno. I guess she's about average.

                                        (CONTINUED)

MATTRESS GUY #1
Average? Hey, man. Average is dumb!

They drop the mattress in place. With the window framing
these guys, the scene FREEZES, looking just like a comic book
panel.

INT. HARVEY'S APARTMENT - DAY

Harvey turns around from the scene and ponders it. He moves
back towards his pile of stick-figure drawings.

CLOSE ON PAPER

Harvey scribbles the words "AMERICAN SPLENDOR" at the top of
the page.

CUT TO:

INT. CLEVELAND DINER - 1975 - DAY

The following scene is shot through the restaurant window. We
see reflections of people walking by.

A tense HARVEY stares at CRUMB as he eats a burger and reads
Harvey's mock-ups. Harvey doesn't touch his burger deluxe and
nervously talks in his laryngitis-afflicted voice.

                    HARVEY
          See, ever since I read your stuff,
          man I've been thinking I could write
          comic book stories that were different
          from anything being done.

                    CRUMB
               (munching on a fry)
          Uh-huh.

                    HARVEY
          I'm thinkin', the guys who do animal
          comics and super-hero stuff are really
          limited 'cause they gotta try to
          appeal to kids. And underground
          comics like yours have been really
          subversive or opened things up politi-
          cally. But there is still plenty more
          ta be done with 'em, too, y'know?

                                              (CONTINUED)

                        CRUMB
          Pass me the ketchup?

                        HARVEY
          I mean with pictures and words, it
          could be more of an art form. Like
          those French movies are. Or De Sica
          over in Italy, y'know? ... So I tried
          writin' some things about real life.
          Stuff the everyman's gotta deal with.

Crumb finally looks up from Harvey's work.

                        CRUMB
          These are about you.

                        HARVEY
          Er, yeah ...

                        CRUMB
          You turned yourself into a comic hero?

                        HARVEY
          Sorta, yeah. But no idealized shit.
          No phony bullshit. The real thing,
          y'know? Ordinary life is pretty
          complex stuff.

Crumb reads more. Harvey waits anxiously. Finally Crumb
starts to chuckle.

                        CRUMB
          These are really good, Harv.

                        HARVEY
                    (insecure)
          Really? Ya think so?

Crumb shuffles through more.

                        CRUMB
          Yeah. This is great stuff, man. I dig
          it. Can I take them home and illus-
          trate them?

Harvey is practically bursting.

                        HARVEY
          Wow!!!

Harvey's voice breaks like a kid in puberty. He clears his throat. And something miraculous happens...

When Harvey opens his mouth to speak his LARYNGITIS IS GONE!

> HARVEY (CONT'D)
> You'd do that for me, man? That'd be great! I can't draw a straight line!

> CRUMB
> Hey, what's up with your voice, Harv? All of a sudden it sounds fine.

> HARVEY
> (thrilled)
> I don't know, man. I guess you cured me!

INT. V.A. HOSPITAL - SNACK ROOM HALLWAY - DAY

HARVEY bounds towards the snack room where a group of hospital workers and patients hang out. He bangs on the window to get their attention. When they look up, Harvey waves a comic book in the air.

                                             DISSOLVE TO:

INT. - V.A. HOSPITAL - SNACK ROOM --DAY

A GLOSSY, FULL-COLOR COMIC BOOK FEATURING THE TWO MATTRESS GUYS: Scrawled across the top in big red letters reads, "AMERICAN SPLENDOR. Vol. #1"

A man's finger points to the words, "All Stories By Harvey Pekar. Art By R. Crumb."

The comic book sits atop a table in the dreary snack room. A crowd of HOSPITAL WORKERS, PATIENTS, DOCTORS, MAINTENANCE WORKERS, etc. (under ten total) gather around a proud HARVEY who shows off his work. For the first time, he seems almost happy.

> HARVEY
> (Beaming)
> See that? All stories by yours truly.

A WWII VET PATIENT with a portable IV cranes to get a glimpse.

                                             (CONTINUED)

                    WW II VET PATIENT
          Hot off the presses, huh? We got a
          regular Hemingway here.

                    HARVEY
          No way, Jack, I don't go in for that
          macho crap.

DOCTOR #3 chimes in.

                    DOCTOR #3
          I didn't know you could draw, Pekar.

                    HARVEY
          Nah! I don't draw. I just write the
          stories. A buddy of mine and some of
          his friends do the art work.

TOBY, the supernerd from the bus stop, grabs the comic book
off the table and peruses it.

                    TOBY
          Harvey, am I in here? You promised I
          would be in here.

                    HARVEY
          Yeah! Yeah! You're in there, alright?
          Jeez, Toby.

SUDDENLY, MR. BOATS -- Harvey's philosophical co-worker --
pushes his way through the crowd. He snatches the comic out
of Toby's hand.

                    MR. BOATS
          Let me see this.

                    TOBY
          Mr. Boats, it's not polite to grab
          things. Next time--

                    MR. BOATS
          Son, you done good. Ya know, I was
          up in Toronto a few weeks back an' I
          saw the Red Chinese Ballet...

As Mr. Boats talks, the crowd starts to disperse.

                         MR. BOATS (CONT'D)
              Now that was beautiful. The way
              those people were dancing together.
              Those Chinese work hard. I tell ya,
              they work hard -- Where is everybody
              goin'?

Mr. Boats hands the comic book to Harvey and turns on his
heels. Through the window he notices TWO VETS IN WHEELCHAIRS
moving down the hall.

                         MR. BOATS (CONT'D)
              Where these sickly men rushin' off
              to? They ain't goin' nowhere for now.
              Maybe not for a long time. But damn
              if they ain't in a rush to get there.

Harvey stands there, his moment of glory passed. But it's
okay. He flips through his comic and smiles.

                                              CUT TO:

EXT. STREET CORNER - ASSOC. OF POLISH WOMEN - 1975 - DAY

A motley group of GUYS hang out on a street corner in front
of the Association of Polish Women. HARVEY heads towards
them.

                         MARTY
              Hey look guys, here comes Captain
              America.

Harvey rolls his eyes.

                         PAHLS
                    (yelling out)
              You gonna hang with the boys now that
              yer a comic book star?

Harvey turns red. He's embarrassed but part of him loves the
attention.

                         HARVEY
              Cut it out. Man, I ain't nothin' yet
              compared to Bob Crumb.

                         GUY #3
              Ah, listen to him. One lousy comic
              book and he wants to be Crumb.

The GUYS laugh.

ANGLE ON SILENT GUY

A SILENT GUY crouches by the wall, reading his CLEVELAND
BROWNS trading cards.

> PAHLS
> Hey Harvey, if ya wanna make comics
> for adults, ya oughtta put some dirty
> stuff in it.

> GUY #3
> Yeah, you can write about Marty's sex
> life.

Harvey hangs with the guys but he doesn't engage. He seems to
be observing them more than interacting with them.

> GUY #3 (CONT'D)
> Right Marty? I heard ya went out wit
> Bonnie yesterday.

> PAHLS
> Yeah. Howdja do? Wudja git offa her?

> MARTY
> Ah, lousy. All's I got wuz arm-
> around.

The guys all stare at him for a moment. Then they crack up.

>   CUT TO:

INT. SOUND STAGE - PRESENT - DAY

HIGH DEFINITION VIDEO DOCUMENTARY FOOTAGE

CLOSE UP:

A COPY OF AMERICAN SPLENDOR #2: A FULL-COLOR CARTOON VERSION
OF THE ABOVE SCENE GRACES THE COVER.

A MARTY LOOK-ALIKE is bombarded with questions about his date
with Bonnie. He complains that all he got was "arm-around."

The REAL HARVEY holds the above comic book in his hand. The stage is set with a few items that indicate a comic book store. HARVEY talks about a couple of "American Splendor" issues and how they impacted his life -- recognition as a writer, etc. He gives his philosophy about the comic book, etc.

The REAL JOYCE is there with him, contradicting him. We learn that comics brought them together.

A MONTAGE OF AMERICAN SPLENDOR COVERS (ISSUE #3, #4, #5, #6 ETC.) THEY INDICATE A PASSAGE OF TIME ...

                                                    CUT TO:

INT. HARVEY'S CUBICLE - V.A. HOSPITAL - 1980'S - DAY

HARVEY sits alone in his cubicle. He doodles stick figures on a pad -- some ideas for a new comic. His posture's miserable. He rubs his temples like he's in anguish.

                    REAL HARVEY (V.O.)
          Here's our man eight comics later, a
          brand new decade, same old bullshit.
          Yeah sure, he gets lots of recognition
          for his writin' now. Sure his comics
          are praised by all the important media
          types tellin' people what to think.
          But so what? It's not like he makes a
          livin' at it like Bob Crumb. He can't
          go an' quit his day job or nothin'.

JUMP CUT SEQUENCE

Several shots of Harvey just thinking, scratching his face with a pencil, tapping his foot nervously. Each shot is sepa-rated by a second or two of black (an homage to Harvey's wordless panels). Finally, he goes back to writing.

                    REAL HARVEY(V.O.) (CONT'D)
          Who am I kiddin'. Truth is I'd be
          lost without my work routine.

                                               FLASH CUT TO:

INT. HARVEY'S BEDROOM - 1980'S - NIGHT

Alone in bed, Harvey wakes up in a cold sweat from a night-mare. He looks horrified, short of breath.

                                               (CONTINUED)

                         HARVEY
                  (calming himself down)
         I got a job ... I got a job ...

                                                 BACK TO:

INT. HARVEY'S CUBICLE - V.A. HOSPITAL - 1980'S - DAY

HARVEY scratches his head.

CLOSE UP ON HIS DOODLING

Harvey writes "I got a job" in a balloon over the stick figure's head.

                         REAL HARVEY (V.O.)
                  So -- to stave off desperation and
                  feelings of uselessness -- I resigned
                  myself to a menial existence. But hey,
                  maybe the guy who's had a happy life
                  feels worse just before he dies than
                  th' guy who had a sad one. Or, maybe
                  not. I dunno. Maybe I just needed a
                  woman.

Toby comes in, decked out in plaid and stripes. He has an
empty messenger bag.

                         TOBY
                  Hi, Harvey. Do you want these gourmet
                  jelly beans? I gave up sweets for
                  lent.

Harvey turns around. He seems down, depressed.

                         HARVEY
                  Huh? Sure, I'll take 'em.

Toby watches Harvey eat a few.

                         HARVEY (CONT'D)
                  Hey, watermelon. That's pretty good.

                         TOBY
                  I recommend the piña coladas. They are
                  excellent and very authentic tasting.

Toby heads down a file row and proceeds to take a few off the
shelves, stuffing his bag. Harvey gets up and comes after him.

                                                 (CONTINUED)

                    HARVEY
          Hey Toby, can you eat lentils during
          lent?

                    TOBY
          Sure. I don't see why not. You can't
          eat meat on certain days, but lentils
          should be acceptable anytime.

                    HARVEY
          Ya think there's any connection
          between lentils and lent?

                    TOBY
          I don't think so but I'll ask Sister
          Mary Fred at church on Sunday.

                    HARVEY
          Sister Mary Fred, huh? Is she cute?
          Sounds kinda mannish but who am I to
          be picky.

                    TOBY
          Harvey, you're funny. She's a nun.

                    HARVEY
          So what? Maybe she became a nun
          because she couldn't get a guy.

                    TOBY
          Harvey, she became a nun because she
          had a higher calling.

                    HARVEY
          Higher calling. That is such a crock
          of shit. I don't know why you waste
          your time prayin' anyway.

                    TOBY
          Well, Harvey, I like the ritual. And
          I'm a very spiritual person. You
          know, you should try believing in
          something bigger than yourself. It
          might cheer you up.

Toby turns on his heels and walks off.

(CONTINUED)

                          HARVEY
                    (calling after him)
              What? Do I seem depressed, Toby?

Toby doesn't respond.

Harvey shrugs and digs deep into the jelly bean bag. He
pulls out a fistful.

CLOSE ON HARVEY'S HAND

Jellybeans in every imaginable color. Harvey fingers a few
and then picks a blue one.

                    BOB THE DIRECTOR (V.O.)
              Cut!

                                                       CUT TO:

INT. - V.A. HOSPITAL "SET" - PRESENT - DAY

HIGH DEFINITION VIDEO DOCUMENTARY FOOTAGE

A few items from the previous scene are present on the sound
stage indicating that it's a set of AMERICAN SPLENDOR -- The
Movie.

THE ACTOR HARVEY stands alone, his hand filled with Jelly beans.

                    BOB THE DIRECTOR
              Okay, that was great. The bakery
              scene is next ...

ACTOR HARVEY steps out of the frame, revealing a craft service table behind him. At the table, the REAL HARVEY and the
REAL TOBY load up on donuts. The two discuss the food on the
set. Ironically, the Real Toby is actually more extreme than
the Actor who plays him -- even more robotic, and completely
incapable of eye-contact.

The REAL TOBY discusses the finer points of nerdom and evaluates the Actor's nerd quotient. The Real Harvey explains to
Actor Toby that nothing -- not even gourmet jelly beans --
would have cheered him up at that point in his life. He was
too lonely and depressed.

END HIGH DEFINITION VIDEO DOCUMENTARY FOOTAGE

                                                       CUT TO:

INT. HARVEY'S BEDROOM - 1980'S - MORNING

Light pours through the curtained window.

Naked and disheveled, HARVEY tosses and turns in bed.

> REAL HARVEY (V.O.)
> My loneliness was unbearable, man.
> Weekends were the worst. Sometimes in
> my sleep, I'd feel a body next to me
> like an amputee feels a phantom limb.

EXT. PEDESTRIAN BRIDGE -- DAY

Extreme wide shot: a city-street overpass spans across the
entire frame. The lone figure of Harvey sulks there in the
middle, watching traffic pass below.

REAL HARVEY (V.O.)
Sure my comics were bringin' me notoriety, but my personal
life was in shambles. I thought a little attention would make
me feel better. It only made me feel worse.

                                                    CUT TO:

EXT. BAKERY SIDE STREET - SPRING - 1980'S - MORNING

It is a beautiful, sunny day. The trees are in bloom.
There's the first scent of spring in the air. Kids play in
the street. Music pours out of passing cars. Everyone seems
to have a smile on his or her face except HARVEY. He walks on
the shadowy side of the street.

EXT. BAKERY STREET - SPRING

Establishing shot of HARVEY trudging into the bakery.

INT. BAKERY - SPRING - 1980'S - MORNING

A couple of WOMEN order bread and cookies from TWO COUNTER
GIRLS.

HARVEY surveys the donuts.

> COUNTER GIRL #1
> (yelling to Harvey)
> Next!

                                              (CONTINUED)

                         HARVEY
                    (to the Counter Girl)
               Yeah! I'll have two crullers, a jelly
               donut with powdered sugar... And you
               got any "day old bread"?

A woman with attractive Irish looks brushes past Harvey on
her way to the door. This is ALICE QUINN, roughly Harvey's
age but there is a tired, weary look in her eyes.

Suddenly, she stops and turns back to Harvey.

                         ALICE
               Hey, you're Harvey Pekar.

Half in a daze, Harvey stares at the chick.

                         HARVEY
               Yeah...

                         ALICE
               Alice Quinn. From school.

Harvey studies her face. Suddenly, it clicks.

                         HARVEY
               Oh yeah. College. We had a couple lit
               classes together.

Harvey pays and receives his items. They step back towards
the door.

                         ALICE
               What happened to you? You just disap-
               peared after one semester.

Harvey scratches his armpit.

                         HARVEY
               I know, man. I got good grades and
               all but there was this required math
               class. I can't do math, an' that
               required class hangin' over my head
               made me crazy. Eventually the pressure
               got to be too much.

                         ALICE
               Well, you're doing okay anyway. I heard
               all about your jazz reviews and your comics.

                                              (CONTINUED)

This perks Harvey up.

                    HARVEY
          Ya did?

                    ALICE
          Sure, your famous. Meanwhile I got my
          degree but I'm just a plain old wife
          and mother.

Harvey stares at her wedding ring. His face drops.

                    HARVEY
          Yeah. I'm not doing as great as ya
          think. My second wife divorced me and
          I work at a dead end job as a file
          clerk. Sometimes I hang out with the
          guys on the corner but most of the
          time I just stay home by myself and
          read.

Alice laughs.

                    ALICE
          You're luckier than you think. My
          husband and kids make it impossible
          for me to cuddle up with a good book.

                                              CUT TO:

EXT. BAKERY - SPRING - 1980'S - DAY

HARVEY and ALICE continue their conversation as they stroll
towards her car.

                    HARVEY
          I'm reading this book by Dreiser now
          -- JENNIE GERHARDT.

                    ALICE
          That's one of my favorites.

                    HARVEY
          I hope it don't end like so many a'
          those naturalist novels... with some-
          one getting crushed ta earth by forces
          he can't control.

Alice smiles.

                                          (CONTINUED)

                         ALICE
          I think you'll be pleasantly sur-
          prised. It's certainly not a Holly-
          wood happy ending, but it's pretty
          truthful. Which is rare these days ...

This hits home with Harvey. He can't believe he's made such
a connection with this woman.

Alice stops in front of a beat-up station wagon.

                         ALICE (CONT'D)
          This is me.

                         HARVEY
          Nice car. I don't have one yet.

                         ALICE
          Can I give ya a lift somewhere?

                         HARVEY
          Nah. It's a nice day. I'll just walk.

Harvey looks down, a little sad.

                         ALICE
          Well, we should have you over some-
          time for dinner.

                         HARVEY
          Sure, I'd be glad t'come. But if you
          really wanna do me a favor, introduce
          me to some a' your single girlfriends.
          I bet they're all smart like you. I'm
          no catch, though, so I'll take any-
          thing you can get me.

Alice pecks Harvey on the cheek.

                         ALICE
          I'll work on it.

She gets into the car.

                         ALICE (CONT'D)
          Nice seeing ya Harvey.

Harvey watches as she drives off.

                                                      (CONTINUED)

                        REAL HARVEY (V.O.)
            When I got home, I finished reading
            JENNIE GERHARDT. It was real good,
            way better than I expected. That
            Alice wuz right.

                                                          CUT TO:

INT. HARVEY'S LIVING ROOM - SPRING - 1980'S - NIGHT

The room is moody, dark and lonely. The shadowy figure of
Harvey sits on the floor devouring JENNIE GERHARDT.

                        REAL HARVEY (V.O.)
            Sure Lester -- the main character --
            croaks in the end, but at least he's
            old and dies a natural dignified
            death.

THE CAMERA TRAVELS AROUND THE ROOM TO FIND: Harvey again, now
silhouetted in the door frame, still clutching the book and
obsessed by his thoughts.

                        REAL HARVEY (V.O.) (CONT'D)
            I was more alone that weekend than
            any. All I did was think about JENNIE
            GERHARDT an' Alice Quinn an' all the
            decades of people I have known.

THE CAMERA TRAVELS AGAIN TO FIND Harvey sitting on a chair in
the corner of his room. His head is bowed. His shoulders
slump over, as if he's struggling with something weighty.

                        REAL HARVEY (V.O.) (CONT'D)
            The more I thought, the more I felt
            like cryin'; Life seemed so sweet an'
            so sad an' so hard t'let go of in the
            end.

THE CAMERA TRAVELS A FINAL TIME TO FIND: Harvey sprawled
across his couch. But he's not asleep; he's still obsessing.
The book lies on his chest like a lover.

Close up of Harvey's troubled face. Beneath the pain, we see
hope and determination.

                         REAL HARVEY (V.O.) (CONT'D)
                    But hey, man. Every day's a brand new
                    deal, right? Just keep on workin' and
                    sump'n's bound ta turn up.

                                                              CUT TO:

EXT. COSMIC COMICS STORE - DELAWARE - 1980'S - DAY

An urban comic book shop on a dicey but bohemian street. A
title over picture reads, "MEANWHILE, IN DELAWARE."

INT. COSMIC COMICS - 1980'S - DAY

JOYCE BRABNER, a depressive nudge with a perpetually peptic
expression frantically searches the store for something. Her
partner, a granola type named RAND, finishes unloading a
stack on the shelf.

                         JOYCE
                    What happened to the new American
                    Splendor?

                         RAND
                    We sold 'em, babe.

                         JOYCE
                    All of them?

                         RAND
                    Yep.

                         JOYCE
                       (accusatory)
                    Damn it! I put one aside for myself,
                    next to the register. I didn't even
                    get a chance to read it.

                         RAND
                    Whoa, sorry, Joyce. I didn't know you
                    were such a Splendor fan. Next time
                    take it home.

Joyce leans against the counter. She pushes up her glasses
and looks really upset.

                                                          (CONTINUED)

                         JOYCE
          Maybe I'll call the publisher. But
          they take so damn long. Shit! Why
          does everything in my life have to be
          such a complicated disaster ...

Joyce starts slamming things around the store. Finally Rand
grabs his stuff.

                         RAND
          Okay, I'm gonna hustle before the
          vibe in here gets any worse.

Rand leaves. Joyce barely notices, still brewing.

                                                    CUT TO:

INT. JOYCE'S BEDROOM - 1980'S - NIGHT

The mess in this room rivals Harvey's. A few cats add to the
clutter. Joyce lies on her disheveled bed and writes a letter.

                         JOYCE (V.O.)
          Dear Mr. Pekar,
          Greetings from the second smallest
          state in the union, an endless plas-
          tics and nylon plantation controlled
          by giant chemical corporations.

                                                    CUT TO:

EXT. HARVEY'S APARTMENT - VESTIBULE - 1980'S - DAY

HARVEY takes his mail out of the box. He finds an oddly deco-
rated envelope.

                         JOYCE (V.O.)
          To make matters more dismal, there
          are no decent comic book stores in my
          town, which is why my partner and I
          opened one ourselves.

                                                    CUT TO:

INT. HARVEY'S BATHROOM - 1980'S - DAY

HARVEY finishes reading the letter sitting on the toilet. A
cat runs around him.

                                                 (CONTINUED)

                         JOYCE (V.O.)
          Despite our steadily faltering busi-
          ness, my partner managed to sell the
          last copy of American Splendor #8 out
          from under me. I'm a big fan and I
          hate to wait for a new order. Is
          there any way I can get it from you
          direct? Sincerely, Joyce Brabner.

Harvey scratches his head. He mutters to himself.

                         HARVEY
          ... man, she's got good lookin' hand-
          writin' ...

INT. HARVEY'S BEDROOM - 1980'S - NIGHT

BEGIN MONTAGE -- HARVEY AND JOYCE COMMUNICATING

We see Harvey in his bed writing.

                         HARVEY
          Dear Joyce,
          Thanks for the letter. Whattya do
          besides sellin' comics?

THE SCREEN SPLITS TO ACCOMMODATE:

INT. DELAWARE PRISON CLASSROOM - 1980'S - DAY

We see Joyce standing in front of a GROUP OF PRISONERS.

                         JOYCE (V.O.)
          I'm a sometime activist and I teach
          writing to prisoners. I try to help
          them build an interior life and make
          art out of their monotonous, suffocat-
          ing routine.

THE SCREEN GIVES WAY TO ANOTHER FRAME

INT. BUS - 1980'S - DAY

HARVEY scribbles a letter while riding on the bus.

                         HARVEY (V.O.)
          Sounds familiar. So you married or
          what?

INT. JOYCE'S APARTMENT - 1980'S - DAY

Joyce empties her can of cat food in a plate and slides it towards her kitty.

                    JOYCE (V.O.)
          I'm divorced, thank god.

INT. HARVEY'S BEDROOM - 1980'S - EVENING

Now we see Harvey (full screen) in bed in his underwear talking on the PHONE. He's clipping his toe nails.

                    HARVEY
          Look, I think you an' I got a lot in
          common. How am I gonna get you to
          come visit me in Cleveland?

                    JOYCE (V.O.)
          Cleveland? You think that's a good
          idea?

                    HARVEY
          It's a great idea. You should meet
          me, 'cause I'm a great guy. Despite
          the way my comics read, I got a lot
          of redeeming characteristics.

CLIP! He clips off a big one.

THE SCREEN SPLITS TO REVEAL

INT. JOYCE'S APARTMENT - 1980'S - NIGHT

Joyce sits on her equally disheveled bed dunking a tea bag. Her hair is wet from a shower.

                    JOYCE
          I don't know. Where would I stay?

                    HARVEY (V.O.)
          With me. Don't worry, I'm not gonna
          put no moves on you or anything.

                    JOYCE
          I'm not worried about that ...
                    (fumbling with a tea cup)
          Hold on, I just spilled chamomile tea
          all over my bathrobe.

(CONTINUED)

                         HARVEY (V.O.)
               So what are ya worried about then?

Joyce sighs and lies down. A variety of AMERICAN SPLENDORS
are across her bed. Different interpretations of Harvey stare
up at her.

                         JOYCE
                       (sipping)
               Well, the way all those different
               artists draw you, I don't quite know
               what to expect. I mean sometimes you
               look like a younger Brando, but then
               the way Crumb draws you -- like a
               hairy ape with all those stinky, wavy
               lines radiating off your body -- it's
               kind of scary.

                         HARVEY (V.O.)
               Those are motion lines. I'm an active
               guy. Anyway, just come out here an'
               I'll try to be anyone you want me ta
               be.

Joyce smiles for the first time.

                         JOYCE
               That's a dangerous offer. I'm a noto-
               rious reformer ...

                                                      CUT TO:

INT. AIRPORT - ARRIVALS GATE - 1980'S - DAY

A nervous JOYCE walks off the plane into the arrivals area.
She scans the crowd of friends, family, lovers and limo dri-
vers waiting to meet the disembarking passengers. Where is
Harvey? What will he look like?

As Joyce surveys the unfamiliar faces, she imagines different
versions of an animated, illustrated Harvey among the people.

She double-takes as sees the R. CRUMB HARVEY -- hairy, scary,
smelly and picking his nose. Joyce rubs her eyes.

Next she sees the BRANDO HARVEY (Gary Dumm), but unfortunately he disappears fast.

                                                   (CONTINUED)

Disappointed, Joyce notices the realistic DREW FRIEDMAN HAR-
VEY walking towards her. She smiles as he dissolves into:

                    HARVEY (O.S.)
          Hey. Are you Joyce?

Joyce turns around. The flesh and blood HARVEY PEKAR stands
before her -- not quite as bad as the Crumb version, not
quite as good as the Dumm version, but still acceptable. She
sighs with relief.

                    JOYCE
          Hi, Harvey. We finally meet in per-
          son.

She politely offers her hand. Harvey shakes it, but he looks
overwhelmed, worried and pessimistic.

                    HARVEY
          Hiya. Look, before we get started with
          any of this, ya might as well know
          right off the bat. I had a vasectomy.

Joyce lets go of his hand. She stares at him in disbelief.

                                                    CUT TO:

INT. TGIF STYLE RESTAURANT - 1980'S - NIGHT

The most awkward date in history. Seated in an ultra-yuppie
restaurant filled with business lunchers, Harvey and Joyce
hide behind their menus. While everyone else looks slick and
successful, these two compete for world's worst posture.

                    HARVEY
          What's wrong?

                    JOYCE
          Nothing.

                    HARVEY
          Somethin's wrong. Yer lookin' around
          everywhere.

                    JOYCE
          I guess I never imagined you eating
          in a place like this.

                                              (CONTINUED)

                         HARVEY
            Me? I never been here. I thought
            you'd like it. But obviously ya don't,
            do ya?

                         JOYCE
            It's fine. What difference does it
            make?

Harvey shakes his head, feeling more pessimistic.

                         HARVEY
            I dunno. None, I guess. (beat)
            They sure got a lot of meat on this
            menu.

                         JOYCE
            You're a vegetarian?

                         HARVEY
            Kinda. I mean ever since I got a pet
            cat, I couldn't eat animals anymore.

Joyce grabs a bread stick.

                         JOYCE
            Hmm. I support and identify with
            groups like PETA, but unfortunately
            I'm a self-diagnosed anemic. Also, I
            have all these food allergies to veg-
            etables that give me serious intes-
            tinal distress. I guess I have a lot
            of borderline health disorders that
            limit me politically when it comes to
            eating.

Harvey just stares at her.

                         HARVEY
            Wow. Yer a sick woman, huh?

                         JOYCE
            Not yet. But I expect to be.
            Everyone in my family's got some kind
            of degenerative illness.

A cheery waitress bounces over.

                                              (CONTINUED)

                    WAITRESS
                  (sing song)
          Good afternoon! I'm your server Cindy!
          What can I bring you two today?

They slowly look up at her.

                                                    CUT TO:

INT. HARVEY'S APARTMENT - 1980'S - NIGHT

JOYCE and HARVEY enter the apartment. The place is a mess, as
usual.

                    HARVEY
          Look, I was gonna clean up, but why
          should I give you any false notions?
          The truth is I got a serious problem
          with cleanliness. I could wash a dish
          ten times and it'd still dirty. They
          even kicked me outta the Army 'cause
          I couldn't learn ta make a bed.

Joyce puts down her bag.

                    JOYCE
          I've seen worse.

She slumps down on the sofa as if she's been here a million
times. She rubs her head. Harvey sits next to her.

                    JOYCE (CONT'D)
          Harvey, go get me water and a few
          aspirin.

Harvey just bounces back up and obeys.

                    HARVEY
          What, ya got a headache?

                    JOYCE
          No, but I want to avoid one.

Harvey empties the aspirin bottle in his palm. For some reason, he's feeling more comfortable.

                    HARVEY
          Well lemme tell ya Joyce, it sure is
          nice ta have company. I mean, despite
          all your problems, you seem like a
          great person. An' hey, sorry if my
          dating skills are kinda rusty, but
          I've just been through hell and back
          with women. I mean that last one
          turned out to be a real nasty bitch.

Harvey arrives back with the aspirin. He hands it to Joyce.

                    JOYCE
          I had a nice time with you, too.

Joyce swallows the pill. Harvey sits down next to her.

                    HARVEY
          Yeah? You had a nice time?

                    JOYCE
          Don't make people repeat themselves.
          It's annoying.

                    HARVEY
          Oh, sorry.

They're inches away from each other.

                    JOYCE
          C'mere ...

She pulls him close. Harvey plants a kiss on her.

They slowly separate. Joyce's eyes are closed. She likes him.
He kisses her again. They start making out, moaning a bit.

But before it gets heavy--

                    JOYCE (CONT'D)
          Harvey?

                    HARVEY
          Yeah?

Joyce opens her eyes. She looks uneasy.

                    JOYCE
          Which door's the bathroom?

                                                        CUT TO:

INT. HARVEY'S APARTMENT - BATHROOM DOOR - 1980'S - DAY

Harvey stands by the bathroom door, despondent. From inside
we hear the sounds of moaning and flushing.

                    HARVEY
          Hey, Joyce! What's wrong? What is it?

                                                        CUT TO:

INT. HARVEY'S BATHROOM - DAY

FLUSH! Joyce is doubled over on the toilet. She's looking
green.

                    JOYCE
          Ugh! I don't know. I think that yup-
          pie food did me in.

                                                        BACK TO:

INT. HARVEY'S APARTMENT - BATHROOM DOOR - DAY

OUTSIDE THE DOOR

                    HARVEY
          I feel terrible. Lemme at least do
          something for you.

                                                        BACK TO:

INT. HARVEY'S BATHROOM - DAY

Joyce gets to her feet and puts her glasses back on. She
picks up a can and sprays air freshener around the room. Then
she looks at the can and realizes it's WD-40.

                    HARVEY
          Can I make ya something? How about
          some chamomile tea?

Joyce puts the can down.

                    JOYCE
          Chamomile tea? What the hell's a guy
          like you doing with that? I thought
          you drink soda pop for breakfast.

                                                     (CONTINUED)

> HARVEY (O.S.)
> I dunno. I noticed you drank a lot of
> it when we started talkin' on the
> phone. So I stocked up on herbal teas
> for your visit.

Joyce turns her head to the door. She's truly surprised by
what Harvey's just said. And very moved. She smiles to her-
self.

                                                      BACK TO:

INT. HARVEY'S APARTMENT - BATHROOM DOOR - DAY

Harvey stands there waiting.

> HARVEY (CONT'D)
> The girl at the Food Co-op picked me
> out all kinds of herbal stuff. One of
> 'ems good for stomachaches. Grandma
> Bear's Tummy Mint, I think.
> Are you still there?

Joyce slowly opens the door. She leans against the door frame
like she's just been through a war.

She takes off her glasses and cleans them with her shirt.

> JOYCE
> Harvey, we better skip this whole
> courtship thing and just get married.

                                                      CUT TO:

INT. HARVEY'S BEDROOM - 1980'S - DAY

Harvey and Joyce are in bed, lying in each other's arms. They
look quite contented.

> HARVEY
> Man, am I glad I talked you into
> comin' up here. Any more time alone
> and I mighta lost it fer good.

> JOYCE
> Me too.

                                                      (CONTINUED)

                              HARVEY
                    So you don't have any problems with
                    movin' to Cleveland?

                              JOYCE
                    Not really. I find most American
                    cities depressing in the same way.

                              HARVEY
                    An' yer okay with the vasectomy thing?

She shrugs.

EXT. PARKING LOT - V.A. HOSPITAL - 1980'S - DAY

HARVEY approaches the building. Instead of dragging his feet
like usual, he seems to be floating on a cloud. We haven't
seen Harvey this happy since... well, since never.

He stops by a junker car and peeks in the window, finding
TOBY eating lunch alone. He has an entire White Castle smor-
gasbord spread across the front seat.

Harvey knocks on the window. Toby rolls it down.

                              HARVEY
                    Ay Toby.

                              TOBY
                         (mouth full)
                    No you can't have any of my White
                    Castle hamburgers so please don't even
                    ask.

                              HARVEY
                    Can I have a fry?

Harvey reaches for a handful of Toby's fries.

                              TOBY
                    Okay, but just a couple, Harvey. I'm
                    not going to eat dinner until very
                    late and this has got to hold me
                    over.

Harvey leans in, always amused by Toby. He steals another
fry.

                                                        (CONTINUED)

                              HARVEY
                         (munching)
                    Whattya got, a church function?

                              TOBY
                    No, I'm driving to Toledo to see a
                    movie. Would you like to come?

                              HARVEY
                    Nah. I gotta fly to Delaware tonight.
                    I'm gettin' married.

                              TOBY
                    Oh. Why Delaware?

                              HARVEY
                    The chick I'm marryin' is from
                    Wilmington. Plus, I gotta help her
                    move her stuff here.
                         (a beat)
                    Why you drivin' ta Toledo to see a
                    movie?

                              TOBY
                    It's not playing at the Mapletown.
                         (a beat)
                    I didn't know you had a girlfriend,
                    Harvey.

                              HARVEY
                    Yeah. We met last week.

Harvey opens the car door and slides in with Toby.

                              HARVEY (CONT'D)
                    Toby, what movie could possibly be
                    worth drivin' 260 miles round trip
                    for?

                              TOBY
                    It's a new film called "Revenge of
                    the Nerds." It's about a group of
                    nerd college students who are being
                    picked on all the time by the jocks,
                    so they decide to take revenge. I
                    already saw it once.

                              HARVEY
                    Wow, ya really dig this movie.

                    TOBY
        I like it a lot, Harvey.

                    HARVEY
        What are these nerds like? How would
        you describe them?

                    TOBY
        Hmm... Nerds are smart but they look
        and act differently than other people.
        Like nerds might wear polyester button-
        down shirts and flood pants where
        their ankles and their socks are
        showing.

Toby spills some catsup on his polyester button-down shirt.
He stands up to get a napkin, revealing his flood pants.

                    HARVEY
        So what yer sayin' is you identify
        with those nerds?

                    TOBY
                (rubbing out the catsup)
        Yes, I consider myself a nerd. And
        this movie has uplifted me. There's
        this one scene where a nerd grabs
        the microphone during a pep rally
        and announces that he is a nerd and
        that he is proud of it and stands
        up for the rights of other nerds.
        Then, he asks the kids at the pep
        rally who think they are nerds to
        come forward ... So nearly everyone
        in the place does. That's the way
        the movie ends.

                    HARVEY
        So the nerds won, huh?

                    TOBY
                (smiling)
        Yes.

Harvey grabs the rest of Toby's fries and opens the door to
leave.

                         HARVEY
              Wow. You got this movie an' I'm get-
              tin' hitched. We both had a good
              month, huh?

                         TOBY
                    (finishing his last burger)
              Right. Harvey, how long are you going
              to be in Delaware because I'd really
              like to see this movie with you?

                         HARVEY
              I'm only goin' for a week but then
              I'll have a wife, so I'll have to
              take her along. Is it a girl flick?

                         TOBY
              Depends on the girl. What kind of
              girl is your new bride? Is she a
              nerd?

                         HARVEY
              I don't know, man. Maybe. She's into
              herbal teas.

Toby watches Harvey saunter off. He returns to his last ham-
burger.

                                                      CUT TO:

EXT. MOVIE THEATER - 1980'S - NIGHT

A brightly lit marquee reads, "REVENGE OF THE NERDS."

The doors to the theater open and a crowd pours onto the
street.

HARVEY, JOYCE and TOBY are among them. Toby proudly wears a
"Genuine Nerd" button on his striped shirt.

                         JOYCE
              I agree with Toby. I think it's a
              story of hope and tolerance.

                         TOBY
              Yes. It's about time that the people
              who get picked on get to be the
              heroes.

                                                   (CONTINUED)

Harvey scrunches his face in disbelief.

> HARVEY
> It's an entertaining flick an' I can
> see why you like it Toby, but those
> people on the screen ain't even sup-
> posed to be you! They're college
> students whose parents live in big
> houses in the suburbs. They're gonna
> get degrees, get good jobs and stop
> being nerds.

Joyce hits Harvey.

> JOYCE
> Harvey, what did I say about loud
> talking? Use your inside voice.

> HARVEY
> (whispering loudly)
> Look Toby, the guys in that movie are
> not 28-year-old file clerks who live
> with their grandmothers in an ethnic
> ghetto.

> JOYCE
> That's enough, Harvey.

> HARVEY
> They didn't get their computers like
> you did -- by trading in a bunch of
> box tops and $49.50 at the supermar-
> ket.

Joyce folds her arms in disapproval. Toby starts to laugh.

> TOBY
> You're funny Harvey.

Harvey looks at him, disappointed. He shakes his head.

> HARVEY
> Sure, Toby. Go to the movies and day-
> dream, but "Revenge of the Nerds"
> ain't reality. It's just Hollywood
> bullshit.

                                        CUT TO:

EXT. TOBY'S CAR -- A FEW MOMENTS LATER

ANGLE ON TOBY'S CAR (through windshield)

Toby and Joyce continue to analyze the movie in the front
seat as Toby starts the ignition.

                                                    CUT TO:

INT. TOBY'S CAR

ANGLE ON HARVEY IN BACK SEAT

Slouched, grumpy and alone on the back seat, Harvey's still
annoyed by the movie.

                     REAL HARVEY (V.O.)
               Okay, maybe I was bein' so harsh on
               Toby onna count a' my own problems.
               Y'see, I wasn't even married a month
               and my old lady was already showin'
               signs a' trouble. Granted, I tend ta
               get married fast 'cause I'll take any
               woman that'll have me, but this time
               I really met my match ...

                                                    CUT TO:

INT. REHEARSAL STUDIO - PRESENT - DAY

HIGH DEFINITION VIDEO DOCUMENTARY FOOTAGE A few items indicating film production are in the frame.

At a table in the foreground, BOB THE DIRECTOR discusses the
character of Joyce with the ACTRESS playing her. The actress
just nods as the director goes on.

We can see THE REAL JOYCE sitting with THE REAL HARVEY in the
distance.

                     DIRECTOR
               Okay, I think the thing with Joyce is
               that as manic as Harvey can be, she
               matches him with depression. In that
               way they complete each other. I mean,
               she's obviously a very smart woman,
               but she has a lot of trouble func-
               tioning in a world she can't control.
                     (MORE)

                                                  (CONTINUED)

                              DIRECTOR (CONT'D)
                    And she's totally obsessed with all
                    things negative; y'know, diseases,
                    dysfunctions, etc.

THE REAL JOYCE and REAL HARVEY listen curiously -- sometimes
pleased, sometimes displeased -- as their personalities are
dissected and boiled down to a few phrases.

CLOSER SHOT OF REAL JOYCE AND HARVEY

The REAL JOYCE puts in her two cents about the actress playing her. She rants about what it's like to be portrayed in a
movie, and having a character arc imposed on her life.

She moves into talking about her relationship with Harvey,
and the first years of their marriage -- how impossible it
was to live with him.

The REAL HARVEY just rolls his eyes.

END HIGH DEFINITION VIDEO DOCUMENTARY FOOTAGE

                                                        CUT TO:

INT. HARVEY'S LIVING ROOM - 1980'S - DAY

JOYCE is on a cleaning rampage. She rummages through piles
upon piles of records while HARVEY paces nervously.

                              JOYCE
                    What about these 78's, Harvey? Can't
                    you sell them to one of those collec-
                    tors?

                              HARVEY
                    Are ya kidding? No way, man. I ain't
                    getting rid of my 78's.

Joyce throws down the records in frustration. Harvey runs
over to check if they're scratched.

                              JOYCE
                         (angry)
                    Forget it then. I give up! How can I
                    make more storage space, if you won't
                    get rid of anything?

                                                        (CONTINUED)

                         HARVEY
          I'll get rid of stuff. Just not my
          good stuff.

                         JOYCE
          Everything's your good stuff. How am I
          supposed to live here, if there's no
          room for me?

                         HARVEY
          Aw come on, baby. I'll make room for
          ya. You just have to give me time.
          I'm not so good at these kind of
          things.

                         JOYCE
          That's because you're obsessive com-
          pulsive Harvey.

A DOOR BUZZER rings. Harvey slams it to unlock the front.

                         HARVEY
          C'mon. I don't wanna hear that psycho-
          babble crap!

                         JOYCE
          I don't care if you wanna hear it or
          not. You're the poster child for the
          DSM III. I'll have you know that I
          come from a very dysfunctional family.
          I can spot personality disorders a
          mile away...

A KNOCK ON THE DOOR interrupts their argument.

Joyce storms away to answer it.

ANGLE ON THE DOOR:

Joyce opens it to face a smiling TOBY -- dressed as usual in
a loud polyester fashion don't. He talks in his strange
robotic voice and avoids all eye contact.

                         TOBY
              Hello Joyce. Is Harvey home?

Joyce turns to Harvey and points to Toby.

                         JOYCE
                 Borderline autistic!

This scene shrinks into a square up in the corner. The next
few scenes (NEUROSIS MONTAGE) further divide up the full
screen like a comic book.

INT. CLEVELAND COMIC BOOK STORE - 1980'S - DAY

R. CRUMB leaps from behind an autograph table (where he's
signing comics) to hop on the back of ZAFTIG BABE, who offers
him a piggy-back ride.

Joyce turns to Harvey.

                         JOYCE
                 Polymorphously Perverse.

                                                    CUT TO:

EXT. PARKING LOT - V.A. HOSPITAL - 1980'S - DAY

JOYCE picks up Harvey from work. HARVEY enters the car, wav-
ing goodbye to the ranting MR. BOATS.

She points to Mr. Boats.

                         JOYCE
                 Paranoid Personality Disorder.

INT. HARVEY'S LIVING ROOM - 1980'S - DAY

THE TELEPHONE RINGS. A disheveled, tired-looking JOYCE flips
through a novel and lets the machine pick up.

                    ANSWERING MACHINE
                 Please leave a message. (Beep)

                         HARVEY
                      (into phone)
                 Hey Joyce, it's me. You're not gonna
                 believe this but some LA producer
                 called an' he wants to do a play
                 about my life. Call me! (click)

Joyce flips the page.

                         JOYCE
                      (to herself)
                  Delusions of grandeur.

END NEUROSIS MONTAGE (return to full screen)

                                                      CUT TO:

INT. THEATER - 1980'S - EVENING

HARVEY and JOYCE sit in a packed theater watching a play.
Joyce looks exhausted.

ANGLE ON STAGE

A STAGE ACTOR HARVEY and a STAGE ACTOR JOYCE share a couch on
the sparse stage.

                    STAGE ACTOR HARVEY
                  See, I think comics can be an art
                  form. With pictures an' words, a guy
                  can pretty much do anything!

                    STAGE ACTOR JOYCE
                  That's true, Harvey. But I didn't come
                  all the way from Delaware to talk
                  about comics ...

The "Stage Actor Joyce" lunges over and plants a kiss on him.

ANGLE ON HARVEY AND JOYCE IN AUDIENCE

Harvey digs it but Joyce looks disgusted.

BACK TO STAGE

We now see STAGE ACTOR HARVEY clutching a tea cup, as STAGE
ACTOR JOYCE kneels before a toilet bowl. Off to the side of
the stage, A SPOT LIGHT illuminates a GUITAR PLAYER, who adds
music to the scene.

                                                      CUT TO:

INT. AIRPORT - 1980'S - DAY

HARVEY and JOYCE walk through the terminal. Harvey brims
with energy but Joyce looks exhausted.

                    REAL HARVEY (V.O.)
          If ya think readin' comics about yer
          life seems strange, try watchin' a
          play about it. God only knows how
          I'll feel when I see this movie. But
          truth be told, the play wasn't half
          bad, and we got a free trip outta it.
          Things were goin' pretty good for a
          change. VARIETY called me "The Blue
          Collar Mark Twain," and Doubleday was
          interested in publishing an anthology
          of "American Splendor."

                                                CUT TO:

INT. AIRPORT - BAGGAGE CLAIM - 1980'S - DAY

Harvey nervously taps his foot as he waits for the bags.
Joyce leans against the carousel staring at a YOUNG MOTHER
with a BABY in a Bjorn.

                    HARVEY
          I hate checkin' bags, man. It always
          takes forever.

He checks his watch. Joyce remains quiet and distant.

                    HARVEY (CONT'D)
          Jesus, look at the time. The bus is
          gonna leave soon and there won't be
          another one for an hour. That means I
          gotta shell out an extra thirty bucks
          for a cab.

Harvey spots a bag that he thinks is his.

                    HARVEY (CONT'D)
          Hey wait, there's our --
                    (a well-dressed man grabs it)
          Figures. That lucky Yuppie's gonna get
          on the bus in time.

Suddenly, Joyce mumbles something to Harvey.

                    JOYCE
          Y'know Harvey, vasectomies are
          reversible.

                                            (CONTINUED)

                    HARVEY
                 (ignoring her)
          Damn Yuppies get everything.

                    JOYCE
                 (raising her voice)
          Are you listening to me? I said
          vasectomies are reversible.

Heads turn.

                    HARVEY
          What? Whattya talkin' about? I don't
          want kids. An' I came clean about my
          vasectomy the first time I set eyes
          on ya', right here in this airport.

More heads turn.

                    JOYCE
          I know but things have changed. I
          think we can be a family.

                    HARVEY
          Family?! What kinda family could we
          possibly be? I ain't no good with
          kids. I can barely take care of
          myself.

                    JOYCE
          I'll take care of the kid and you.

                    HARVEY
                 (dead serious)
          No way Joyce. Forget it. I can't do
          it; I can't have no kids.

Joyce folds her arms... dejected, defeated. The audience of
eavesdroppers looks disappointed as well.

                                             CUT TO:

INT. HARVEY'S LIVING ROOM - 1980'S - DAY

If the place was a disaster before, believe it or not, it's
gotten worse. JOYCE seems to have given up on her organiz-
ing... and everything else for that matter.

                                             (CONTINUED)

HARVEY hysterically searches through the mess for a record album. Joyce just lies listlessly on an open futon on the middle of the room; it looks as if she hasn't been up in days.

                    HARVEY
          Where the hell is that Ornette Coleman
          album, Joyce? I got a review due
          tomorrow.

Joyce rolls over.

                    JOYCE
          I didn't touch it, Harvey. Would you
          let me sleep?

                    HARVEY
          But it's one o'clock! How late can a
          person sleep?

Joyce sits up. This time she means business.

                    JOYCE
          It happens to be Saturday you selfish
          sonofabitch! And don't you go telling
          me what to do. I'm the one who moved
          into your city, into your home, into
          your vasectomy and into your screwed-
          up life. The least you could do is
          allow me to live here my way.

She rolls over and covers her head with the pillow. Harvey just stands there staring at her.

                                        CUT TO:

INT. SUPERMARKET - 1980'S - DAY

                    REAL HARVEY (V.O.)
          I tried everything but nothin' could
          get this woman outta bed.

HARVEY peruses the aisles. He pulls box upon box of herbal tea off the shelves.

                    REAL HARVEY (V.O.) (CONT'D)
          I mean she wouldn't get a job, wouldn't
          go out, wouldn't make friends, nothin'.

                                        CUT TO:

INT. HARVEY'S LIVING ROOM - 1980'S - DAY

HARVEY throws boxes of herbal teas at JOYCE as she sprawls
listlessly on the futon. She just yawns and turns over on
her side.

                    REAL HARVEY (V.O.)
          Joyce diagnosed herself as "clinically
          depressed." I don't know what the
          hell she was goin' through but it was
          sure takin' it's toll on me.

A frustrated Harvey tries once more to cheer her up.

                    HARVEY
               (upbeat)
          We can go out for dinner tonight. How
          'bout catching a bite at Tommy's?

                    JOYCE
               (mumbling)
          I'm not hungry.

Harvey throws his hands in the air and walks off.

                    HARVEY
          I give up.

As he passes the answering machine, he notices it's blinking.

                    HARVEY (CONT'D)
          Hey Joyce, we got a message here. Why
          didn't you pick up.

Joyce doesn't respond.

                    HARVEY (CONT'D)
          Useless.

He presses the play button.

ANGLE ON ANSWERING MACHINE: A loud "beep," then ...

(CONTINUED)

                         MALE VOICE
            Hi, this is a message for Harvey
            Pekar. My name is Jonathan Greene
            and I'm a producer for LATE NIGHT
            WITH DAVID LETTERMAN. We'd like to
            talk to you about coming on the show
            to plug your comics. Please give me
            a call at 212-555-3333.

                         HARVEY (O.S.)
            What the hell?

Joyce sits up. Harvey's finger hits the "Replay" button.

                         MALE VOICE
            Hi, this is a message for Harvey --

                                                    CUT TO:

EXT. MANHATTAN SKYLINE - 1980'S - DAY

ESTABLISHING SHOT

The impressive skyline glistens in the spring sun.

                         REAL HARVEY (V.O.)
            Joyce finally got off the futon...

                                                    CUT TO:

EXT. WASHINGTON SQUARE PARK - NEW YORK - 1980'S - DAY

Armed with shopping bags from Bleecker Bob's Record Shop, the
Strand Book Store and Forbidden Planet Comic Book Emporium,
HARVEY and JOYCE eat lunch on a park bench. Harvey chomps on
a knish and watches oddball New Yorkers stroll by as Joyce
nibbles on her hot dog.

                                                    CUT TO:

INT. HOTEL HALLWAY -- DAY

CLOSE UP ON AN ICE BUCKET

Cut back to reveal Harvey, schlepping an ice bucket down a
hall in his underwear. A FEMALE BUSINESS TRAVELER passes and
stares at him. He enters a room with a "DO NOT DISTURB" sign.

INT. NEW YORK HOTEL ROOM - 1980'S - DAY

The PEKARS have already wreaked havoc on their luxury hotel room. It looks like a tornado touched down on the New York Hilton.

HARVEY tries on outfits for the big show. He pulls a wrinkled T-shirt over his head and models it for JOYCE who is spread out on the bed surrounded by piles of clothing, scissors and sewing supplies. She glances up at Harvey's get-up and shakes her head no.

                    HARVEY
          Aw, c'mon. Who the hell cares?

Harvey tosses his shirt over to Joyce, who snatches it and starts cutting it with a scissor.

                    HARVEY (CONT'D)
          Hey, whattya doin?

                    JOYCE
          Merchandising.

She resumes her mysterious sewing project; she seems to be making some kind of doll.

                                        CUT TO:

INT. GREEN ROOM - NBC STUDIOS - 1980'S - DAY

Backstage, JOYCE watches LATE NIGHT WITH DAVID LETTERMAN on a monitor as HARVEY awaits his turn to go on camera. He has changed out of his wrinkled T-shirt into a slightly more for-mal look -- a denim shirt and a ratty seersucker striped jacket.

LETTERMAN SHOW - STOCK FOOTAGE

ANGLE ON MONITOR (Note: This is actual stock footage of the show)

A 1980's DAVID LETTERMAN wisecracks.

INT. GREEN ROOM - NBC STUDIOS - 1980'S - DAY

Neither Joyce nor Harvey look particularly impressed with the whole deal.

                                        (CONTINUED)

                         JOYCE
              People like this show?

Harvey paces.

                         HARVEY
              I'm gettin' hungry back here. They
              oughtta leave ya donuts or somethin'.

A nervous STAGE MANAGER wearing a headset peeks his head in.

                         STAGE MANAGER
              Dave's ready for you now, Mr. Pekar.

                         HARVEY
              Hey, you got anything ta eat? My
              stomach's growling.

                         STAGE MANAGER
                    (checking his watch)
              There's no time to eat now.

Harvey glances at the monitor just as Letterman announces his
next guest.

LETTERMAN SHOW - STOCK FOOTAGE

                         LETTERMAN
              Okay. Our next guest works as a file
              clerk in a Cleveland hospital.

INT. GREEN ROOM - NBC STUDIOS - 1980'S - DAY

The stage manager grabs Harvey by the arm. Joyce stops them.

                         JOYCE
              Wait a minute. Where's the doll?

                         HARVEY
              He's got it at the desk. Will you
              relax about that already?

                         STAGE MANAGER
              Guys, guys, we're in a hurry here.

The Stage Manager physically pushes Harvey out of the Green
Room. Joyce turns back to face the monitor.

LETTERMAN SHOW - STOCK FOOTAGE

ANGLE ON MONITOR

Letterman holds up a copy of a full-size glossy AMERICAN
SPLENDOR ANTHOLOGY.

> LETTERMAN
> ... He also writes comic books which
> detail his day-to-day pains and pleas-
> ures, and this is an anthology of
> nine of those comics. It's entitled
> AMERICAN SPLENDOR... From off the
> streets of Cleveland, please say hello
> to Harvey Pekar.

*THE HARVEY PEKAR WHO WALKS ONTO THE SET IS NOT THE ACTOR POR-
TRAYING HIM BUT RATHER THE REAL HARVEY PEKAR (only about 15
years younger). THIS IS ACTUAL STOCK FOOTAGE FROM HARVEY'S
FIRST LETTERMAN APPEARANCE.*

INT. GREEN ROOM - NBC STUDIOS -- DAY

Joyce watches as Harvey shakes Letterman's hand and takes a
seat.
LETTERMAN SHOW - STOCK FOOTAGE

He smiles as the audience warmly greets him. It seems
Harvey's grooving on this attention. But as soon as the
audience quiets down, Harvey turns to his host and starts his
offensive:

> HARVEY
> I'm ready for those Cleveland jokes.
> Go ahead...

Taken off guard, Letterman laughs.

> LETTERMAN
> Alright settle down Harvey. Settle
> down.
>   (the Audience laughs)
> Now let's explain to folks who may
> not be familiar with your work what
> it is you do here, exactly. You have
> comic books about you in your daily
> life in Cleveland.

> HARVEY
> That's right.

                              LETTERMAN
                    And are they embellished at all or is
                    it pretty much factual?

                              HARVEY
                         (patronizing)
                    No. It's all true, David. All true.

                              LETTERMAN
                    And you also have a regular job in
                    Cleveland working at a hospital.

                              HARVEY
                    That's right. Aiding the sick, yes.

                              LETTERMAN
                    Aiding the sick. Well that's certainly
                    noble work.

                              HARVEY
                    Thank you. Thank you.

INT. GREEN ROOM - NBC STUDIOS - 1980'S - DAY

ANGLE on Joyce watching

                              JOYCE
                         (unimpressed)
                    Such brilliant repartee ...

                                                            BACK TO:

LETTERMAN SHOW - STOCK FOOTAGE

                              LETTERMAN
                    Now it seems to me Harvey that you
                    have a very successful career here.
                    This is being published by a major
                    publishing company, Doubleday. Why do
                    you maintain the day job?

                              HARVEY
                         (defensive)
                    To make a living!
                         (big laughs)
                    I don't make a living as a writer.
                    I've been writing for many years,
                    David. Maybe more years than you've
                    been alive.

                                                          (CONTINUED)

Now, Letterman cracks up.

                                                  BACK TO:

INT. GREEN ROOM - NBC STUDIOS - 1980'S - DAY

A LETTERMAN REGULAR (Tony Randall?) comes in with some food.
He stops by the monitor to watch a moment with Joyce.

                    HARVEY
          Yeah, I know that my youthful appear-
          ance belies, you know, my actual age.
          But, I've been around for a long
          time--

                    LETTERMAN REGULAR
               (to JOYCE)
          You know this guy?

                    JOYCE
          I'm beginning to wonder.

The Letterman Regular takes a seat as he watches the monitor.
He seems more intrigued than Joyce.

LETTERMAN SHOW - STOCK FOOTAGE

                    LETTERMAN
          But I have a feeling though, if you
          wanted to, you could probably get by
          on what you make selling your work.
          Because I know people are after you
          to write other things. You're publish-
          ing this anthology...

This hits a sore spot. Harvey goes from politely condescend-
ing to cantankerous in one second flat!

                    HARVEY
          Who? What people? What people? What
          are you talking about? Where the hell
          do you get that stuff?

Letterman cracks up. The Audience laughs even harder.

                    HARVEY (CONT'D)
          I'm no show biz phoney. I'm telling
          the truth. Come on, man.

                                             (CONTINUED)

The Audience can't believe this guy's holding his own with
Letterman.

INT. GREEN ROOM - NBC STUDIOS - 1980'S - DAY

ANGLE ON LETTERMAN REGULAR

                    LETTERMAN REGULAR
               (to Joyce)
          At least he's keeping up with
          Letterman.

                    JOYCE
          Pandering is more like it.

Suddenly, Joyce walks over to the monitor and looks for the
channel. She hits a button, but it only changes the frame of
the show.

                    JOYCE (CONT'D)
          Dammit.

                    LETTERMAN REGULAR
          Excuse me, but what are you doing?

                    JOYCE
          I'm trying to get some news. You know
          there's a big story about to break
          about the US selling arms to Iran and
          the Contras.

                    LETTERMAN REGULAR
          That's a monitor.

                    JOYCE
          Ugh. Just forget it.

Joyce gives up. She sinks back into her seat and pulls a book
from her bag. The Letterman Regular stares at her like she's
from Mars.

LETTERMAN SHOW - STOCK FOOTAGE

ANGLE ON THE MONITOR

                    LETTERMAN
          Harvey, I know you've got a job. I've
          got a job. We're both very lucky. We
          both have jobs.

                                                (CONTINUED)

                    HARVEY
          Then what's the matter?

Once again laughs and a big round of applause. Letterman
pulls out Joyce's mysterious doll and props it up on the
table.

                    LETTERMAN
          We've gotta go. Harvey I like you.
          I'm on your side. I enjoy the comic
          books. And here, quickly tell us about
          the little doll here.

                    HARVEY
          My wife made it.

INT. GREEN ROOM - NBC STUDIOS - 1980'S - DAY

BACK TO JOYCE.

She suddenly perks up.

                    JOYCE
          Finally something good.
                    (to Letterman Regular)
          Watch this.

LETTERMAN SHOW - STOCK FOOTAGE

CLOSE-UP OF THE DOLL

It is an absolutely horrific but oddly evocative "Harvey Rag
Doll." His face is inspired by Crumb's drawings of Harvey
but even more extreme. His little T-shirt reads, "American
Splendor."

The Audience is in stitches.

                    LETTERMAN
          They're made out of your old clothing.

                    HARVEY
          That's right.

                    LETTERMAN
          And what do these go for?

                    HARVEY
          Thirty-four bucks.

                                                        (CONTINUED)

                              LETTERMAN
                          (shocked)
                    Thirty-four dollars? Thirty-four dol-
                    lars for this?

                              HARVEY
                    What are ya cheap. You cheaper than
                    me?

                              LETTERMAN
                    Would you pay thirty-four dollars for
                    that?

                              HARVEY
                    No but I'm not asking it. My wife is.

                                                      BACK TO:

INT. GREEN ROOM - NBC STUDIOS - 1980'S - DAY

JOYCE stares at the monitor, expressionless. The STAGE MAN-
AGER sticks his head in.

                              STAGE MANAGER
                    He's a natural.

                              LETTERMAN REGULAR
                    He is. Good stuff.

The Stage Manager grabs the Regular.

                              STAGE MANAGER
                    C'mon. Your turn.

A smiling HARVEY (the actor now) waltzes in straight from his
command performance.

                              HARVEY
                    Whad'ya think?

Joyce taps her finger on Letterman's image on the monitor.

                              JOYCE
                    Megalomanic.

                                                  DISSOLVE TO:

INT. NEW YORK HOTEL ROOM - 1980'S - DAY

HARVEY tries on a ripped T-shirt for Joyce who lies on the
bed.

> REAL HARVEY (V.O.)
> It became clear pretty fast that I
> was invited on the show just for
> laughs. But what the hell did I care?
> Letterman was an okay guy. Let him
> take pot shots at me, s'long as I got
> paid an' got to plug my comics.

                                        CUT TO:

LETTERMAN SHOW - STOCK FOOTAGE

MONTAGE: A series of actual HARVEY appearances on LATE NIGHT
WITH LETTERMAN.

INT. GREEN ROOM - NBC STUDIOS - 1980'S - DAY

JOYCE, whose different outfits reflect time passage, watches
each time from the GREEN ROOM.

LETTERMAN SHOW - STOCK FOOTAGE

ANGLE ON MONITOR

HARVEY, in a ratty T-shirt, spars with LETTERMAN.

> LETTERMAN
> Harvey, you are the embodiment of the
> American dream ...

The Audience laughs.

> REAL HARVEY (V.O.)
> Funny thing is, somethin' about me and
> Letterman clicked for the viewers. He
> kept wantin' me back.

LETTERMAN SHOW - STOCK FOOTAGE - ANOTHER SHOW

LETTERMAN introduces his favorite guest.

                                        (CONTINUED)

> LETTERMAN
> It is my pleasure to welcome back our
> next guest, the lovable Harvey Pekar!

HARVEY walks out with a box of donuts. He starts giving
Letterman an earful right off the bat.

> REAL HARVEY (V.O.)
> Here was this slick, ambitious guy
> with millions, winnin' over the coun-
> try by makin' light of everything.
> And then there was me... A messy
> loser with no dough who takes every-
> thing too seriously.

> LETTERMAN
> Tell me Harvey, what do you do to get
> away from the pressures of being --
> well, a file clerk? (laughter)

> HARVEY
> Go ahead and laugh, folks. But he has
> more contempt for you than I do!

> CUT TO:

INT. WHITE CASTLE - 1980'S - DAY

The burger joint has been transformed into a film set with
lights, cameras and lots of trendy MTV types.

> REAL HARVEY (V.O.)
> An it wasn't just me gettin' all the
> attention. As a result of my appear-
> ances on Letterman, my buddy Toby
> Radloff landed a gig for MTV
> extolling the virtues of White Castle
> burgers...

OFF TO THE SIDE:

Two HOT BABES slave over TOBY at he gets his hair and make-up
done.

HARVEY wanders onto the set. He finally spots Toby in the
corner. As he heads over to say hello, Harvey bumps into the
MTV DIRECTOR -- a new wave fashion victim who looks like a
lost member of A FLOCK OF SEAGULLS.

> (CONTINUED)

                         MTV DIRECTOR
              Christ! Watch where you're going!

                         HARVEY
                         (muttering)
              Fuckin' yuppie or whatever kinda freak
              you are.

                         REAL HARVEY (V.O.)
              That day on the set with those MTV
              jerks, I had an epiphany. It seemed
              that real, salt of the earth people
              like Toby an' me were bein' coopted
              by these huge corporations. We were
              gettin' held up and ridiculed as los-
              ers in the system. What can I say, it
              was the 80's man.

                                                        CUT TO:

MTV PUBLIC SERVICE ANNOUNCEMENT

TOBY, dressed in dark sunglasses and a turtleneck, stands in
front of a White Castle. He delivers his lines in his trade-
mark robotic style. There's an MTV logo on the bottom of the
screen.

                         TOBY
              Hamburgers are a safer addiction than
              drugs. Say no to drugs. Say yes to
              White Castle!

                                                        CUT TO:

INT. CLEVELAND DINER - 1980'S - DAY

HARVEY and JOYCE eat breakfast together. Harvey reads a
Katherine Mansfield book as JOYCE reads a newspaper.

                         JOYCE
                         (looking up from the paper)
              Harvey, I've been reading about these
              kids who grew up in war zones --
              Palestinians, Israelis, El
              Salvadorians, Cambodians... These kids
              are amazing and they're --

A YUPPIE in a jogging suit walks up to Harvey, interrupting
Joyce in mid-sentence.

                                                        (CONTINUED)

                    YUPPIE
          Hey, you're that guy from the
          Letterman show, right?

                    HARVEY
               (smiling)
          Yeah, that's me.

                    YUPPIE
          That's so excellent. You and Stupid
          Pet Tricks are a riot.

Harvey's not smiling anymore. This guy's a jerk.

                    HARVEY
          Yeah? Then why dontcha buy one of my
          comics, man. That's the only reason
          I go on that dumb show anyway.

                    YUPPIE
          Right, sure. Later, Harvey Pekar!

The Yuppie rushes out.

                    HARVEY
          Asshole.

                    JOYCE
          Anyway, I want to do a political
          comic book about these kids. There's
          a conference in Jerusalem in a few
          weeks, and I can start by doing
          interviews there.

                    HARVEY
          Whoa whoa, wait a second. Jerusalem? I
          can barely drag you off the futon to
          go to the Letterman show.

                    JOYCE
          Y'know why? 'Cause I don't give a
          damn about the Letterman show. I want
          to work on something important to me.
          Something that matters.

Joyce hit a nerve.

                                        (CONTINUED)

                              HARVEY
                         (furious)
                    Hey! You know I only go on the show
                    for the extra bread!

People start to look over.

                              JOYCE
                    Harvey ... you're yelling ...

                              HARVEY
                    Maybe if you got yer lazy ass up and
                    got a job, I could work on something
                    that matters, too, huh?!

Joyce doesn't dignify Harvey with an answer. She stares at
him, her eyes well with hurt.

He sighs, calming down. He looks around sheepishly.

                         HARVEY (CONT'D)
                    I'm sorry, baby. I -- I'm sorry ...

He grabs her hand.

                                                          CUT TO:

EXT. HARVEY'S APARTMENT - 1980'S - DAY

HARVEY and JOYCE stroll across the lawn holding hands. They
move towards a waiting CAB. Harvey carries his wife's bags.

                         REAL HARVEY (V.O.)
                    I guess it was good ta finally see
                    Joyce excited about somethin' of her
                    own. Sure I was happy for her. But I
                    was still upset for me.

They stop by the cab.

                              HARVEY
                    This is crazy. Can't ya just do some-
                    thin' here in Cleveland?

                              JOYCE
                    Harvey, you'll survive a few weeks
                    alone.

                                                      (CONTINUED)

                              HARVEY
                 Alright ... Be careful. I love you, baby.

They kiss. Harvey grudgingly puts her bags in the car. He
watches as the cab pulls away.

                         REAL HARVEY (V.O.)
                 It was later that night when I first
                 found the lump.

                                                       CUT TO:

INT. HARVEY'S BEDROOM - 1980'S - NIGHT

Wearing only his shorts, Harvey lies alone in the communal
futon, flipping through a book. He reaches into his underwear
to scratch his nuts.

Suddenly he stops. He feels something odd ...

For a moment he just freezes. His eyes register panic.

                         REAL HARVEY   (V.O.)
                 I was determined to put it outta my
                 mind until Joyce got back. Easier said
                 than done.

                                                       CUT TO:

INT. V.A. HOSPITAL - 1980'S - DAY

An enraged HARVEY fights with his co-worker MIGUEL.

                              HARVEY
                 What do I care! Just gimme the chart
                 already!

                              MIGUEL
                 What is your problem today!?

                              HARVEY
                 Look, Miguel! I just don't wanna keep
                 comin' back here for it, okay?!

                              MIGUEL
                 Harvey, that patient's due t'be admit-
                 ted a week from now! Why do you
                 always have to be picking fights with
                 everybody?

                                                    (CONTINUED)

                         HARVEY
                      (yelling)
             How many times do we gotta go through
             the same bullshit. Just gimme the
             fuckin' chart!

Offended, Miguel storms off.

                         MIGUEL
             We'll see what the doctor says about
             this.

                                              CUT TO:

INT. HARVEY'S LIVING ROOM - 1980'S - NIGHT

Alone and slumped over his table, HARVEY draws comic ideas
with stick figures. Nothing's coming to him. He looks like
he's in anguish.

Frustrated, Harvey crumbles the idea and throws it on the
floor. He knocks over a chair.

INT. HARVEY'S BEDROOM - 1980'S - NIGHT

He tosses and turns in bed. No way he's sleeping.

                                              CUT TO:

INT. HARVEY'S LIVING ROOM - 1980'S - DAY

HARVEY is yelling into the telephone. It is a bad connection.

                         HARVEY
                      (loudly into phone)
             Whadya mean? Another two weeks? Ya
             gotta come home some time! Hello?
             DAMMIT!

                                              CUT TO:

INT. BACK STAGE - NBC STUDIOS - 1980'S - DAY

Without Joyce, a surly HARVEY waits in the wings for his
introduction. He sneaks a peek as Letterman finishes up the
"Stupid Pet Tricks" segment. We hear dogs barking and audience laughter.

>   LETTERMAN (O.S.)
>   And there you have it, folks! Another
>   enlightening episode of Stupid Pet
>   Tricks!

>   REAL HARVEY (V.O.)
>   I was startin' ta lose it. Between
>   the lump, the loneliness -- I felt
>   like everything wuz closin' in on me.
>   And with Joyce over there savin' the
>   world, I never felt more like a sell-
>   out hack in my life.

>   LETTERMAN (O.S.)
>   Y'know ladies and gentlemen, when
>   Thoreau wrote that most men lead
>   lives of quiet desperation, he obvi-
>   ously had not met our first guest,
>   who happens to lead a life of whining
>   desperation ...

Harvey clenches his fists.

>   HARVEY
>   (threatening)
>   Okay, asshole. You'll pay fer that
>   one...

Harvey takes off his shirt. He pulls another T-shirt out of
the bag and changes ...

>   LETTERMAN (O.S.)
>   Ladies and gentlemen, please welcome
>   back, Harvey Pekar.

Harvey's new T-shirt reads "ON STRIKE AGAINST NBC." He takes
off for the stage, fists clenched, a soldier marching off to
war.

                                                  DISSOLVE TO:

INT. GREEN ROOM - NBC STUDIOS - 1980'S - DAY

We're positioned behind the monitor, so we can only hear the
show. THE STAGE MANAGER AND TWO PRODUCTION ASSISTANTS
straighten up in the room.

                                                  (CONTINUED)

                         HARVEY (O.S.)
            Hey, Dave! You wanna know what my
            politics are? I'm a strident leftist,
            Dave.

                        LETTERMAN (O.S.)
            I could have guessed half of that.

                         HARVEY (O.S.)
            You coulda guessed all of it, man! So
            why don't we talk about your parent
            comany, G.E., huh? Let's talk about
            anti-trust violations and nuclear
            reactors!

                        STAGE MANAGER
            Joe, put more sodas in the fridge,
            there. And let's clean up the coun-
            ters. That Pekar guy's a pig.

As the P.A.'s walk back and forth in front of the monitor, we
hear the Letterman / Pekar banter grow louder.

Suddenly PRODUCTION ASSISTANT #2 stops and checks out the
monitor.

                    PRODUCTION ASSISTANT #2
            Whoa ... you guys. Check this out.

INT. TOBY'S LIVING ROOM - 1980'S - EVENING

TOBY and his GRANDMOTHER watch HARVEY raise hell on
Letterman. Again, we can't see the screen.

                         HARVEY (O.S.)
            You're a cop-out, Letterman. You're
            nothin' but a shill for G.E.

Toby's GRANDMOTHER passes him a plate of cookies.

                        LETTERMAN (O.S.)
            First of all, Harvey, what you are
            saying is not true. Second of all,
            this is not the place to say it. If
            you want to talk about this, go some-
            where else, because you're not talking
            about it here!!

                                                        CUT TO:

INT. MR. BOAT'S KITCHEN - 1980'S - EVENING

Dressed in a bathrobe, Mr. Boats eats a lonely, late-night
snack (cake and milk) at his kitchen table. A 12" TV on the
table has Harvey and Dave on.

                    HARVEY (O.S.)
          Don't worry, Dave. I won't come back
          unless you beg me.

                    LETTERMAN (O.S.)
          You're not coming back at all.

                    HARVEY (O.S.)
          What do I care--

                    LETTERMAN (O.S.)
          Because we've given you many, many
          chances to talk about things that
          would be of general interest to
          people--

                    HARVEY (O.S.)
          So what?!

Mr. Boats shakes his head.

INT. TOWN CAR - 1980'S - NIGHT

We see Harvey alone, slumped in the back seat of a Town Car,
heading back towards his hotel. City lights pass over his
troubled face. We still hear the show, as if it's now in his
head.

                    LETTERMAN (V.O.)
          --And also to promote your little
          Mickey Mouse magazine. Your little
          weekly reader! But you've blown every
          chance you've got. You're a dork,
          Harvey!

                    HARVEY (V.O.)
          Dave, you're fulla shit! You're fulla
          shit!!

                                        DISSOLVE TO:

INT. HARVEY'S APARTMENT - BEDROOM - 1980'S - NIGHT

CLOSE ON AN AMERICAN SPLENDOR COMIC

The cover depicts a snarling LETTERMAN yelling, "YOU FUCKED
UP A GREAT THING!" at a smirking, self-satisfied HARVEY.

JOYCE lies in bed reading the comic, chuckling. HARVEY cuddles up against her.

                    JOYCE
          I guess you did it this time.

                    HARVEY
          Who cares. He wasn't helpin' my sales
          anyway. (moving closer)
          Baby, don't go away anymore. I just
          can't take bein' alone.

Joyce puts the magazine down.

                    JOYCE
          If you met those kids over there and
          saw what they go through, you wouldn't
          ask that of me.

                    HARVEY
          But If you go again I'm really gonna
          lose it.

                    JOYCE
          It's not open for discussion, Harvey.
          I need this in my life right now.

She cuddles up close to him.

                    JOYCE (CONT'D)
          But I do appreciate the fact that you
          missed me so much. C'mere ...

She starts to kiss him. He kisses her back. Her hands wander
down. Suddenly she feels something strange.

                    JOYCE (CONT'D)
          Harvey, what is that?

Harvey looks at her and gulps.

                                        CUT TO:

INT. HOSPITAL ROOM - 1980'S - DAY

HARVEY and JOYCE sit in the office holding hands, like two
terrified school kids. A DOCTOR stands before them. They just
got bad news ...

> JOYCE
> I don't understand, does "tumor" mean
> the same thing as "cancer"?

The doctor gently nods.

Joyce covers her mouth. Harvey holds onto his head. He looks
positively dizzy.

The doctor starts to talk, yet the words don't seem to match
his mouth. He looks dubbed. Strange phrases just weave
together, echo and bounce off the wall, making no sense at
all.

*... we know the growth is malignant. What we don't know is
how far it may have spread. Once we have the results of the
biopsy, we can make more informed decisions about treatment
... blah, blah, blah ....*

The whole office seems to spin.

> CUT TO:

EXT. HARVEY'S APARTMENT - 1980'S - LATER

Joyce and Harvey sit on the stoop of their apartment house,
in a daze. The words keep echoing around them. Harvey holds
his head.

> DOCTOR #2 (O.S.)
> *... cat scan ... diagnosis ... MRI
> ... cancer ... cancer ... cancer ...*

> HARVEY
> How can I have cancer? I don't feel
> sick at all.

> JOYCE
> That's a positive thing.

(CONTINUED)

                         HARVEY
          My cousin Norman died of lymphoma. He
          was twenty-nine. He was a brilliant
          oncologist.

                         JOYCE
          Stop it! You're not going to die,
          Harvey. You're not.

Harvey turns to Joyce.

                         HARVEY
          What's going to happen to you, baby?
          Who's gonna take care of you if I'm
          not around?

Joyce stands up, determined.

                         JOYCE
          Harvey, look at me and focus. We are
          going to get through this. I under-
          stand illness. I know how to handle
          these things.

                         HARVEY
          But that's you. I'm not strong enough.
          I don't know how ta be positive. I
          can't do it. I can't.

                         JOYCE
          Yes, you can. And I'll tell you how.
          You'll make a comic book out of the
          whole thing. You'll document every
          little detail. And that way you'll
          remove yourself from the experience
          until it's over.

Despite Joyce's passionate pitch, Harvey shakes his head.

                         HARVEY
          I can't do that. I'm just not strong
          enough... I just wanna die.

Joyce folds her arms.

                         JOYCE
          Fine. I'll do it without you.

INT. HARVEY'S BEDROOM - 1980'S - NIGHT

HARVEY and JOYCE lay there quietly, both exhausted. Joyce turns over so her back faces Harvey. He puts his arm around her.

CLOSE ON JOYCE'S FACE

A tear drips down her cheek.

                                        CUT TO:

INT. HARVEY'S APARTMENT - 1980'S - DAY

Joyce is straightening up the apartment. The place actually looks halfway decent.

THE DOORBELL RINGS

Joyce opens the door. A guy in his 30's named FRED -- Hells Angels tough guy meets sensitive artist -- stands at the door. He's accompanied by a seven-year-old girl, DANIELLE.

                    FRED
          Hey, I'm Fred. You called me about
          the comic book?

                    JOYCE
          Right -- the artist. Come on in.

                    FRED
          This is my daughter, Danielle. I had
          to bring her along. I hope you don't
          mind.

Joyce leans down and addresses the girl, who holds a toy horse.

                    JOYCE
          Hi, Danielle. What's that you're hold-
          ing?

                    DANIELLE
          A pony.

It's immediately obvious that Joyce is great with kids.

                    JOYCE
          A pony? What's his name?

                                        (CONTINUED)

>   DANIELLE
>   She's a girl. Clarissa.

>   JOYCE
>   Oh, I see. Well, I'm Joyce. Nice to
>   meet both you and Clarissa.

They all walk towards the table which is covered with papers.

>   FRED
>   I'm really sorry to hear about
>   Harvey. Is he here?

>   JOYCE
>   He's going to work until next week,
>   when he starts the chemo. That's why
>   I wanna get this project started now.
>   Once he's stuck here, I know he'll
>   take over.

>   CUT TO:

EXT. HARVEY'S APARTMENT - 1980'S - LATER

Miserable and in a daze, HARVEY walks up to his front door.
He looks like a man whose days are numbered. When he reaches
the door, he searches his pocket for keys.

ANGLE ON POCKET

Harvey's hand comes up empty.

>   HARVEY
>   Shit!

Harvey tries the doorknob, but it's locked.

He steps back on the lawn and looks around. Could he have
dropped them? He retraces a few steps.

>   HARVEY (CONT'D)
>   Dammit!

Harvey yells up at the window.

>   HARVEY (CONT'D)
>   Joyce, open the door! I lost my keys
>   again! Joyce!!

>   (CONTINUED)

ANGLE ON FRONT DOOR

HARVEY'S ELDERLY NEIGHBOR struggles with her shopping cart
through the door.

Harvey pushes past her to get in.

INT. HARVEY'S APARTMENT VESTIBULE

Harvey knocks again. Nothing. Now he punches the door.

> HARVEY
> Joyce!! Open the fucking door!!

Suddenly the door opens. Loud music pours out. But it's not
Joyce, it's FRED, the artist.

> FRED
> Hey, Harvey.

> HARVEY
> Fred?

Harvey just stares at him. Fred opens the door to reveal:

JOYCE and DANIELLE dancing together with the stereo blasting.
They're having a ball.

> CUT TO:

INT. HARVEY'S APARTMENT - 1980'S - DAY

At the kitchen table, HARVEY looks over FRED's sketches.
JOYCE and DANIELLE are now building a house of cards on the
living room floor.

> FRED
> Here are some ideas we batted around.

> HARVEY
> Sheesh. Joyce doesn't know what she's
> doing. There's too many words in these
> frames. When are ya comin' back?

> FRED
> Uh, she said something about next
> Tuesday, which is fine with me. Only
> thing is, I might have the kid again.
> (MORE)

                         FRED (CONT'D)
          My ex-wife's supposed to take her,
          but I don't have much faith in her
          showing up. She is in worse shape
          than me these days.

Harvey looks away at Joyce and Danielle playing. They're
oblivious to the world.

                         HARVEY
          Next week my treatment begins. Do me
          a favor. Bring the kid with you.

                                                    CUT TO:

CLOSE-UP: A PENCIL SKETCHING

FRED'S PENCIL completes a sketch of Joyce pushing Harvey in a
wheelchair. The word "cancer" appears everywhere, floating
all around the image.

COMIC ART / REAL LIFE MONTAGE

The following montage chronicles Harvey's illness by cutting
between comic art depicting key events and shots of HARVEY,
JOYCE and FRED creating the book.

The montage is set to the simultaneously dulcet and discordant
tones of Miles Davis' "Blue In Green" (or something similar).

                                                    CUT TO:

INT. HOSPITAL HALLWAY - 1980'S - DAY

Close on Harvey's face as he's getting pushed down the hall
in a wheelchair.

                                                    CUT TO:

M.R.I. COMIC PANEL

A panel of Harvey entering the M.R.I. machine.

                                                    CUT TO:

INT. HARVEY'S APARTMENT - 1980'S - DAY

We see Harvey, Joyce and Fred sitting around a table. Joyce
fights to keep Harvey focused on the project.

                                               (CONTINUED)

                                                    CUT TO:

BACK TO MORE COMIC PANELS:

1) An enraged Harvey throws things around the house.

2) Joyce on the bed crying, a cat licking her back.

                                                    CUT TO:

INT. HARVEY'S SHOWER - 1980'S - DAY

A balding Harvey depressed in the shower. He holds a clump of
hair in his hand.

                                                    CUT TO:

COMIC PANEL OF THE ABOVE SCENE

Harvey in the shower. The balloon above his head reveals his
inner turmoil over losing his hair and his face swelling.

MORE COMIC PANELS FOLLOW

Harvey in agony. Various positions of him in bed, on all
fours, covered with a case of shingles. "I feel like I'm on
fire" appears over his head.

                                                    CUT TO:

INT. HARVEY'S KITCHEN - 1980'S - DAY

Joyce and Fred go over some more comic art. Joyce carries the
idea over to Harvey (wearing a baseball cap), who can't get
out of the couch. He looks it over and nods. Danielle brings
Harvey a glass of water.

                                                    CUT TO:

MORE COMIC PANELS:

Harvey crawling up the steps. "I'm so weak I can't make it,"
he thinks ...

Harvey and Joyce in a hospital waiting room. He's slumped
over, she has her hand on him.

                                                    (CONTINUED)

A delirious Harvey surrounded by nurses and Joyce. "She's torturing me, she won't let me die, I wanna die ..."

CUT TO:

INT. HARVEY'S BATHROOM - 1980'S - DAY

A balding Harvey lies on his bathroom floor. His cat walks all over him.

                    HARVEY
         I wanna die ... just let me die ...

CUT TO:

MORE COMIC PANELS

Joyce attempts to wake Harvey up. She curses at him. She slaps him. "Why are you doing this to me!"

A drawing of Joyce, doubled over, crying. "I can't take this anymore ..."

THE MONTAGE ENDS WITH A SCENE IN HARVEY'S BEDROOM

CUT TO:

INT. HARVEY'S BEDROOM - 1980'S - NIGHT

A repeat of the opening scene ... Like a ghost, a naked HAR-VEY stands over his bed staring down at a sleeping JOYCE. In the eerie light, he's almost translucent.

                    HARVEY
                  (faintly)
         Joyce ... Joyce?

Joyce springs up, alarmed.

                    JOYCE
         What's wrong, Harvey? What are you
         doing up?

Harvey just stands there for a moment saying nothing.

                    JOYCE (CONT'D)
         What is it?

                    HARVEY
              (delirious, out of breath)
         Tell me the truth. Am I some guy who
         writes about himself in a comic book?
         Or am I just --just a character in
         that book?

                    JOYCE
         Harvey ...

                    HARVEY
         When I die, will 'dat character keep
         goin'? Or will he just fade away.

Joyce just stares at him, unsure how to answer. Finally
Harvey collapses.

Joyce leaps from the bed, nervous, hysterical. She gets down
on the floor and shakes him.

                    JOYCE
         Omigod Harvey! Harvey, wake up!

CLOSE ON HARVEY'S FACE

His eyes remain closed, his expression far, far away. The
sound of Joyce's voice fades until it seems like a distant
echo.

Then PANELS from Harvey's comics begin to float over his
head, his life literally passing before his eyes in comic
book form.

Slowly, the comic images and the unconscious Harvey evapo-
rate, giving way to:

GREEN SCREEN

A SURREAL DREAM SEQUENCE

We are now in a large, empty room similar to a blank comic
book panel.

A healthy, fully dressed Harvey appears in the corner of the
frame. He is very far away, barely recognizable. We slowly
dolly towards him as he delivers a formal soliloquy to the
camera:

                                                    (CONTINUED)

                         HARVEY
          My name is Harvey Pekar. It's an
          unusual name -- Harvey Pekar...

As Harvey speaks, one-dimensional comic book images from his
life pass over the screen once again. This time in front of
him, behind him, everywhere. We dolly in towards him.

                         HARVEY(CONT'D)
          1960 was the year I got my first
          apartment and my first telephone book.
          Imagine my surprise when I looked up
          my name and saw that, in addition to
          me, another Harvey Pekar was listed!

Images of Harvey's childhood float by, followed by his young
adult years.

                         HARVEY(CONT'D)
          I was listed as Harvey L. Pekar... My
          middle name is Lawrence... He was
          listed as Harvey Pekar -- no middle
          initial... Therefore, his was a purer
          listing.

We see Harvey age in the images: he's hanging on the street
corner with friends, collecting records, hanging with Crumb.

                         HARVEY (CONT'D)
          Then, in the seventies, I noticed that
          a third Harvey Pekar was listed in
          the phone book! This filled me with
          curiosity. How could there be three
          people with such an unusual name in
          the world, let alone in one city!?

Now, numerous images of Harvey's many years at the V.A.
Hospital float by: Harvey filing, Harvey arguing with his
boss, Harvey and Toby, etc.

                         HARVEY(CONT'D)
          Then one day, a person I worked with
          expressed her sympathy to me concern-
          ing what she thought was the death of
          my father. She pointed out an obituary
          notice in the newspaper for a man
          named Harvey Pekar. One of his sons
          was named Harvey. These were the
          other Harvey Pekars.

                                              (CONTINUED)

The comic images fade out. Harvey is once again alone in the empty room.

                    HARVEY(CONT'D)
          Six months later, Harvey Pekar Jr.
          died. Although I'd met neither man,
          I was filled with sadness. "What
          were they like," I thought. It
          seemed that our lives had been linked
          in some indefinable way.

We slowly move in on his face. Extremely close. As close as the camera can get.

                    HARVEY(CONT'D)
          But the story does not end there.
          For two years later another Harvey
          Pekar appeared in the directory. What
          kind of people are these? Where do
          they come from, what do they do?
          What's in a name?

END DREAM SEQUENCE

INT. HARVEY'S BEDROOM - 1980'S - DAY

BACK TO BEDROOM:

We are close on HARVEY'S face as he lays passed out and delirious on the floor. Over this WE HEAR...

                    HARVEY
          Who is Harvey Pekar?

His face slowly fades to black.

A MOMENT OF BLACK, AND THEN ...

INT. TOWER BOOKS - 1980'S - DAY

FADE IN:

CLOSE UP: A GLOSSY, FULL-COLOR, NOVEL-SIZED COMIC COVER.

Scrawled across the top in yellow and red it read, "Our Cancer Year." The drawing depicts Harvey doubled over on the front lawn, groceries in the snow, with Joyce attempting to help him up.

                                        (CONTINUED)

A hand flips the book open and signs the inside leaf.

JOYCE and a healthy-looking HARVEY sit at a table signing
copies of their opus. About fifteen or so people mill about
with copies.

                    REAL HARVEY (V.O.)
            Here's our man a year later. Somehow
            I made it though the treatments, an'
            the doctors are optimistic. I guess
            Joyce was right about doin' the big
            comic book. We published the thing as
            a graphic novel -- our first collabo-
            ration -- and ended up with rave
            reviews. We even won the American Book
            Award. Go figure ...

                                                        CUT TO:

INT. HARVEY'S LIVING ROOM - 1980'S - DAY

The place is still a mess but somehow it has a better vibe
than it had before. This might be due to the presence of
DANIELLE. She sits crossed legged on the floor making
jewelry out of beads. JOYCE guides her.

HARVEY shuffles into the room. He watches for a moment as
Joyce and Danielle play.

ANGLE ON JOYCE: There is an awkward expression almost resem-
bling a smile on her face. He interrupts them.

                    HARVEY
            Hey Joyce.

Joyce looks up. Harvey looks like he's trying to hide something.

                    JOYCE
            What is it Harvey?

                    HARVEY
            That was the doctor.

Joyce stops what she's doing and gulps. She hangs on
Harvey's every word.

                    HARVEY (CONT'D)
            He said I'm all clear.

                                                   (CONTINUED)

Tears well in Harvey's eyes. Joyce breathes a sigh of relief.
Danielle jumps up and runs over to Harvey. She hugs him.

CUT TO:

EXT. CLEVELAND ICE RINK - 1980 - DAY

HARVEY sits in the bleachers, watching JOYCE teach DANIELLE
to ice skate.

Harvey's got a box of pizza next to him. He picks up a slice
and chomps on it. The cheese drips out of his mouth onto his
shirt.

                    REAL HARVEY (V.O.)
          The weirdest thing that came outta my
          illness was Danielle. With her real
          mother runnin' around who knows where,
          an' seein' how well her and Joyce got
          on, Fred decided she'd have a better
          life with us. I was scared at first
          but then I thought, what the hell.
          She's a good kid. So we ended up
          takin' her an' raising her as our
          own.

CUT TO:

INT. HARVEY'S APARTMENT - 1980'S - DAY

HARVEY and DANIELLE lie on the futon together. Harvey's
comics are strewn around them everywhere. Danielle flips
through one.

                    HARVEY
          Ya keep readin' 'em backward.

                    DANIELLE
          I like reading them backward.
                 (holding up a comic)
          Is that you?

                    HARVEY
          I keep tellin' ya, all of 'ems me,
          man.

                    DANIELLE
          You look like a monster.

                                              (CONTINUED)

                    HARVEY
          Yeah, well wait'll ya see what you're
          gonna look like.

                    DANIELLE
          Me??

                    HARVEY
          Sure. Yer part of the story too, now.

                    DANIELLE
          What story?

                    HARVEY
          The story of my life.

Danielle makes a face.

                    HARVEY (CONT'D)
          Yeah, I know I'm not as interesting
          as The Little Mermaid and all that
          magical crap...

                    DANIELLE
          Maybe I want to write my own comic.

                    HARVEY
          Oh yeah? What about?

                    DANIELLE
          I don't know yet. But not about you.
          You have enough already.

                                               CUT TO:

EXT. SCHOOL BUS STOP - FALL - PRESENT - DAY

HARVEY walks towards the bus stop to send DANIELLE to school.
He holds her hand.

                    HARVEY
          Ya know, you should write about things
          in your own life. Like school and...
          ponies ... I don't know, girl stuff...

                    DANIELLE
                (to Harvey)
          Do you have to hold my hand?

                                            (CONTINUED)

                              HARVEY
                          (wounded)
                What, are you embarrassed a' me? I
                know, I'm embarrassing. I felt the
                same way about my father.

Danielle looks up at Harvey like he's crazy.

                              DANIELLE
                No Harvey. You're just squeezing it
                too hard.
                          (shaking her head)
                Joyce is right. You are obsessive-
                compulsive.

Danielle drops his hand and rushes onto the bus with the
other kids.

Harvey waves and watches as it pulls away.

He turns and walks by himself down the busy Cleveland
street -- a familiar image from the opening. He's still
hunched over. He's still Harvey.

                       REAL HARVEY   (V.O.)
                Yeah, so I guess comics brought me a
                lot. But don't think this is some
                sunny, happy ending. Every day is
                still a major struggle. Joyce an' I
                fight like crazy, an' she barely
                works. The kid's got A.D.D. and is a
                real handful. My expenses have gone up
                so much that I'm writin' freelance
                'round the clock, just to make my
                bills. My life is total chaos.

                                                    DISSOLVE TO:

EXT. BUS STOP - FALL - PRESENT - DAY

DOCUMENTARY FOOTAGE -- SHOT ON FILM

NOW THE REAL HARVEY walks down the same busy Cleveland street
towards his job.

                              REAL HARVEY (V.O.)
              With a little luck, I'll get a window
              of good health between retirin' an
              dyin'. The golden years, right? Who
              knows. Between my pension and the
              chunk of change I got for this movie,
              I should be able to swing somethin'.
              Sure I'll lose the war eventually, but
              the goal is to win a few skirmishes
              along the way. Right?

                                                        CUT TO:

INT. V.A. HOSPITAL - PRESENT - DAY

DOCUMENTARY FOOTAGE -- SHOT ON FILM

THE REAL HARVEY slumps at the desk now, flipping through a
comic book.

ANGLE ON DOOR

THE REAL TOBY comes into the file room, carrying a cake
with sparklers. He's followed by a group of Harvey's REAL
CO-WORKERS and JOYCE and REAL DANIELLE.

Harvey moves the comic off his desk so Toby can put the cake
down.

ANGLE ON CAKE

The festive cake reads "HAPPY RETIREMENT HARVEY."

REAL JOYCE cuts the cake and passes slices to the group.
ANOTHER WORKER pops a bottle of champagne.

CLOSE on a glass of champagne getting filled. The glass sits
next to the comic Harvey was reading.

CLOSE UP ON COMIC BOOK COVER

HARVEY's new edition of AMERICAN SPLENDOR is subtitled, "OUR
MOVIE YEAR." It features an illustration of HARVEY, JOYCE and
DANIELLE surrounded by cameras, lights and crew.

FADE OUT:

STILL PHOTOGRAPHY

"Paniots Nine"
Written by Peter Dolger
Performed by Joe Maneri
Courtesy of Avant Records

"Soul Power"
Written by Captain
Performed by Captain
Courtesy of Killer Tracks

"On The Sunny Side Of The Street"
Written by Jimmy McHugh and Dorothy Fields
Performed by Lester Young & The Oscar Peterson Trio
Courtesy of the Verve Music Group
Under license from Universal Music Enterprises

"Chasin' Rainbows"
Written by Dallas String Band
Performed by R. Crumb And His Cheap Suit Serenaders
Courtesy of Shanachie Entertainment Corp.

"Blue Devil Jump"
Written by Paul Quinichette
Performed by Jay McShann
Courtesy of Atlantic Recording Corp.
By arrangement with Warner Special Products

"Taint Nobody's Bizness (If I Do)"
Written by Everett Robbins and Porter Grainger
Performed by Jay McShann
Courtesy of Atlantic Recording Corp.
By arrangement with Warner Special Products

"Ain't That Peculiar"
Written by Robert Rogers, William Robinson Jr., Marvin
Tarplin and Warren Moore
Performed by Marvin Gaye
Courtesy of Motown Records
Under license from Universal Music Enterprises

"I'll Be With You In Apple Blossom Time"
Written by Neville Flesson and Albert Von Tilzer
Performed by the Andrews Sisters
Courtesy of MCA Records
Under license from Universal Music Enterprises

"Know Your Rights"
Written by Joe Strummer and Mick Jones
Performed by The Clash
Courtesy of Epic Records/
Sony Music Entertainment (UK) Ltd.
By arrangement with Sony Music Licensing

"Stardust"
Written by Hoagy Carmichael and Mitchell Parish
Performed by Dizzy Gillespie
Courtesy of Savoy Records and June St Entertainment

"Escape (The Pina Colada Song)"
Written by Rupert Holmes
Performed by Rupert Holmes
Courtesy of MCA Records
Under license from Universal Music Enterprises

"Hula Medley"
Traditional
Performed by R. Crumb And His Cheap Suit Serenaders
Courtesy of Shanachie Entertainment Corp.

"American Splendor"
Written by Eytan Mirsky
Performed by Eytan Mirsky

"Lady Be Good"
Written by George and Ira Gershwin
Performed by Dizzy Gillespie
Courtesy of Savoy Records and June St Entertainment

"Big Ed"
Written by Mark Cherrie
Performed by Mark Cherrie
Courtesy of Opus One

"Silent Morning"
Written by Noel Pagan
Performed by Noel
Courtesy of the Island Def Jam Music Group
Under license from Universal Music Enterprises

"All Black and White"
Written by Clair Marlo and Alexander 'Ace' Baker
Performed by Studio Musicians
Courtesy of FirstCom Music, Inc.

"My City Was Gone"
Written by Chrissie Hynde
Performed by The Pretenders
Courtesy of Warner Music U.K. Ltd.
By arrangement with Warner Special Products

"My Favorite Things"
Written by Richard Rodgers and Oscar Hammerstein II
Performed by John Coltrane
Courtesy of Atlantic Recording Corp.
By arrangement with Warner Special Products

"Ain't That Peculiar"
Written by Robert Rogers, William Robinson Jr., Marvin Tarplin and Warren Moore
Performed by Chocolate Genius
Courtesy of V2 Records, Inc.

The AMERICAN HUMANE ASSOCIATION monitored the animal action.
No animal was harmed in the making of this film. (AHA 00251)

Cast and Crew Credits

HBO FILMS PRESENTS A GOOD MACHINE PRODUCTION
A FILM BY SHARI SPRINGER BERMAN & ROBERT PULCINI PAUL GIAMATTI HOPE DAVIS "AMERICAN SPLENDOR" CASTING BY ANN GOULDER
MUSIC SUPERVISOR LINDA COHEN MUSIC BY MARK SUOZZO EDITOR ROBERT PULCINI PRODUCTION DESIGNER THÉRÈSE DEPREZ
DIRECTOR OF PHOTOGRAPHY TERRY STACEY LINE PRODUCER CHRISTINE KUNEWA WALKER ASSOCIATE PRODUCER JULIA KING PRODUCER TED HOPE
BASED ON THE COMIC BOOK SERIES "AMERICAN SPLENDOR" BY HARVEY PEKAR AND "OUR CANCER YEAR" BY HARVEY PEKAR AND JOYCE BRABNER
WRITTEN AND DIRECTED BY ROBERT PULCINI & SHARI SPRINGER BERMAN
AMERICA ONLINE KEYWORD: AMERICAN SPLENDOR www.AMERICANSPLENDORMOVIE.COM

CAST
(in order of appearance)

Superman	CHRIS AMBROSE	Real Toby	TOBY RADLOFF
Batman	JOEY KRAJCAR	Counter Girl	BIANCA SANTOS
Robin	JOSH HUTCHERSON	Alice Quinn	MAGGIE MOORE
Green Lantern	CAMERON CARTER	Joyce Brabner	HOPE DAVIS
Young Harvey	DANIEL TAY	Rand	MIKE RAD
Housewife	MARY FAKTOR	Cheery Waitress	AMY K. HARMON
Harvey Pekar	PAUL GIAMATTI	Real Joyce	JOYCE BRABNER
Real Harvey	HARVEY PEKAR	Stage Actor Harvey	DONAL LOGUE
Interviewer	SHARI SPRINGER BERMAN	Stage Actor Joyce	MOLLY SHANNON
Throat Doctor	LARRY JOHN MYERS	Guitarist	EYTAN MIRSKY
Lana	VIVIENNE BENESCH	Stage Manager	ROB GRADER
Nurse	BARBARA BROWN	Letterman Regular	TERRENCE SULLIVAN
Mr. Boats	EARL BILLINGS	MTV Director	EBON MOSS-BACHRACH
Marty	DANNY HOCH	Yuppie	PATRICK LAFFERTY
Robert Crumb	JAMES URBANIAK	Miguel	JESSE PEREZ
Pahls	ELI GANIAS	Talk Show Host	JEFF PETERS
Old Jewish Lady	SYLVIA KAUDERS	PA #1	OLA CRESTON
Cashier	REBECCA BORGER	Cancer Doctor	ROBERT J. WILLIAMS
Mattress Guy #1	NICK BAXTER	Fred	JAMES McCAFFREY
Mattress Guy #2	ALLEN BRANSTEIN	Danielle	MADYLIN SWEETEN
WW II Patient	DICK PROCHASKA	Real Danielle	DANIELLE BATONE
Doctor	CHARLES EDUARDOS	Letterman Regular Voice	JASON STEVENS
Toby Radloff	JUDAH FRIEDLANDER	Talk Show Host Voice	TODD CUMMINGS
Bob the Director	ROBERT PULCINI	Production Supervisor	ANDY WHEELER

CREW

Additional Editing by . . . . . .TIM STREETO
Good Machine
   Production Executive   MELINKA THOMPSON-
                               GODOY
First Assistant Director . . . .CHIP SIGNORE
Location Manager . . . . . . .MICHAEL M. ROCHFORD
Camera Operator . . . . . . .STEVEN DRELLICH
1st Assistant Camera . . . . .OLIVER CARY
2nd Assistant Camera/
   B Camera Operators . . .ALEX ESBER
                          W. KIELY CRONIN
Camera Loader . . . . .IAN L. AXILROD
Camera Interns . . . . .IAN CARMODY
                          ALEX MANGEN
Stills Photographer . . . . . .JOHN CLIFFORD
Script Supervisor . . . . . . .MICHAEL TAYLOR
Sound Mixer . . . . .WHIT NORRIS
Boom Operator . . . . .MICHAEL B. DAVIES
Art Department
   Coordinator . . . . .DEBORAH MARSH
Set Decorator . . . . .ROBERT DESUE
Leadman . . . . .KENNETH KELLERS
On Set Dresser . . . . .DIANA STOUGHTON
Swing Gang . . . . .DONALD J. LIEGL
                          DAVID W. MOONEY
                          ERIKA RICE
                          JOHN CHAMPION
                          JACK GARDNER
                          JAMES E. TODD
Property Master . . . . .MINDY HARRIS
Props Assistants . . . . .LYNN KRAMER
                          DEAN MACUR
Assistant to Production
   Designer . . . . .TEMA LEVINE
Art Department PA . . . . . . .MATTHEW T.
Art Department Interns . . . .BETH O'BRIEN
                          MATT HAUSMANN
                          TODD HECKELER
                          DUSTIN LUCIEN
                          SHAINA MALKIN
                          MIKE O'NEILL
Gaffer . . . . .STEVEN RAMSEY
Best Boy Electric . . . . .RUSSELL O. WULFF
Company Electrics . . . . . . .JULIE ANN "DOC" LINDSTROM
                          LESTER PARKER

Additional Electrics . . . . . .CHUCK COCITA
                          GEORGE McDOUGALL
                          FRANK McKEON
                          CHRISTY TADDEO
                          JOHN TURK
                          RONALD ZABARSKY
Key Grip . . . . .DAN JARRELL
Best Boy Grip . . . . .MATTHEW E. JENNINGS
Dolly Grip . . . . .JOE CASSANO
Company Grips . . . . .KEITH NICKOSON
                          JACK YAGER
Additional Grips . . . . .JOSEPH L. McDERMOTT
                          JONATHAN MEYER
                          MICHAEL F. TAYLOR
                          ADAM WHITE
Costume Supervisor . . . . .MURSHEL C. LEWIS
Key Costumer . . . . .ROBIN K. FIELDS
Costume Assistant . . . . . .KIMBERLEE ANDREWS
Wardrobe Intern . . . . .SARAH SILVER
Makeup Department Head . .LUISA ABEL
Hair Department Head . . . . .R. DEANNA
Additional Hair and Makeup .KATHY MADISON
Hair and Makeup Swing . . . .DEBORAH R. LILLY
Assistant Location Manager .JEREMY BAILEY
Location PA . . . . .JOE CORTESE
Additional Location PA . . . .BECKY WOODWARD
Second Assistant Director . .MERYL STAVITZ
2nd 2nd Assistant Director . .ERIC LASKO
Additional 2nd Assistant
   Director . . . . .MATT G. SHEETS
Set Production Assistants . . .ANDY BETHKE
                          CHAD BRONSON
                          RYAN J. POLACK
                          ELIZABETH ROHRBAUGH
                          DEVON ZEIGLER
Additional Set PA's . . . . . .AMANDA L. PREPUTNIK
                          DAVID LEMOYNE JONES
Production Assistants
   to Cast . . . . .ERIC MUSS-BARNES
                          CHRIS PETRO II
New York Unit Line
   Producer . . . . .DECLAN BALDWIN
New York Unit
   Production Manager . . .CHIP SIGNORE
Bookkeeper . . . . .BRIAN CANTALDI

Legal Counsel . . . . .EPSTEIN, LEVINSON,
BODINE, HURWITZ
& WEINSTEIN LLP
ALISON COHEN
Production Administrative
Supervisor . . . . .ROBERT FEGEN
Production Secretary . . . . .LESLEY WARD-ZICKEFOOSE
Office PA . . . . .JASON GERSTEIN
Assistant to
Christine Walker . . . . .JASON COOPER HALL
Additional Production
Secretary . . . . .JEN O'NEAL
Assistant to Ted Hope . . . . .LAMIA GUELLATI
Clearance Assistants . . . . . .DERRICK KARDOS
BILLY LALOR
Principals Casting Assistant .LIZ BAIRD
Cleveland Extras Casting . . .MARCY RONEN
Extras Casting Assistant . . . .KENDALL EMBRESCIA
Transportation Coordinator . .THOMAS TITUS McCUE
Transportation Captain . . . .WAYNE CONWAY
Drivers . . . . .CHERYL DENNIS
RUSS A. MINERD
Additional Driver . . . . . . .LARRY SPENCER
Picture Car Wrangler . . . . . .ROMAN A. WLASZYN
Craft Service . . . . .VIRGINIA M. HERDMAN
SARA LIEBERTH
Craft Service Assistant . . . .PAULA D. COLLINS
Additional Craft Assistant . . .WILLIAM BALL
Security . . . . .TENABLE SECURITY
Caterer . . . . .PREMIERE CATERERS
Chef . . . . .MICHAEL SANTERAMO
Assistant Chef . . . . .ROBERT LANGHORST
Insurance . . . . .AON/ALBERT G. RUBEN
Payroll Services . . . . .ENTERTAINMENT PARTNERS
Camera, Grip &
Electric Equipment . . . . .PANAVISION
Production Vehicles . . . . . .HADDAD'S
Color by . . . . .DELUXE TORONTO
Production Dailies . . . . . . .DELUXE TORONTO
24 Frame Playback . . . . . .PAT MEEHAN

POST PRODUCTION
Post Production Supervisor . .JULIA KING
Sound Editing . . . . .C 5 INC.
Mix Facility . . . . .SOUND ONE/C 5 INC.
Re-recording Mixer . . . . . . .RON BOCHAR
Supervising Sound Editor . . .NICHOLAS RENBECK

Sound FX Editor . . . . .ALLAN ZALESKI
Dialogue Editors . . . . .ALBERT GASSER
ANNE POPE
ADR Editor . . . . .JEFF STERN
Foley Supervisor . . . . . . .GEORGE A. LARA
Foley Artist . . . . .JAY PECK
Transfer Assistant . . . . . . .CHRIS FIELDER
First Assistants . . . . .ALEXA ZIMMERMAN
RUTH HERNANDEZ
C 5 Office Manager . . . . .ELISABETH GIGLIO
Avid provided by . . . . . . .PIVOTAL POST
Avid Facility Manager . . . .JANELL FLETCHER
Post Accountant . . . . .JENNIFER FREED
TREVANNA POST, INC.
LA Post Production
Supervisor . . . . .JANET ECKHOLM
Post Production
Coordinator . . . . .LINUS HUME
Post Production Intern . . . .MITCHELL GUTMAN
Credit Sequence Stills . . . .IAN CARMODY
Opticals & Digital
to Film Transfer . . . . .HEAVY LIGHT DIGITAL
End Crawl . . . . .DUART DIGITAL
Negative Cutter . . . . .CATHERINE RANKIN
Color Timer . . . . .ALFREDO FRASSON
Animation, Title Sequence
& Visual Effects
Created by . . . . .TWINKLE
Design and Animation . . . .GARY LEIB
Animation and Compositing .JOHN KURAMOTO

The First Live Theatrical Production based on the
comic book "American Splendor"
was produced by The Independent Eye

The Producers would like to thank all those
who kept the hope of AMERICAN SPLENDOR, The Movie,
alive over the years: Bernt Capra, Vince Waldron,
The Arena Stage and Jim Stark

"Our Cancer Year" and "The New American Splendor
Anthology" provided courtesy of
Four Walls Eight Windows

LATE NIGHT WITH DAVID LETTERMAN
courtesy of NBC STUDIOS

The filmmakers wish to acknowledge the creative work of Walt Kelly

Original Artwork Provided by:

DOUG ALLEN
GREG BUDGETT
R. CRUMB
GARY DUMM
JASON GERSTEIN
DEAN HASPIEL
JOE SACCO
GERRY SHAMRAY
FRANK STACK
JOE ZABEL

"Our Movie Year" Artwork by
MARK ZINGARELLI

SPECIAL THANKS:

JUDE BRENNAN	PAUL BRENNAN ESQ.
CHRIS CARMODY	DEBRA GREICO
WAYNE HAROLD	ROBERT KATZ
ADAM SHULMAN	LEWIS PAYTON
MATT LOEB	CARLA RAIJ
ALICIA SAMS	MARY JANE SKALSKI

PAM SMITH

CITY OF CLEVELAND   CITY OF LAKEWOOD
CLEVELAND FILM COMMISSION

CAROL AND JOHN'S COMICS   COLLECTOR'S WAREHOUSE
COMIC WORLD   CONTINENTAL AIRLINES
NORMAN BARR and the DETROIT THEATRE
ELMWOOD BAKERY   GENE'S PLACE
HALLORAN ICE RINK
ANNE KUENZEL and LAKEWOOD HOSPITAL
SHAY'S RESTAURANT   ZONE TRAVEL

ALCO VENDING MACHINES   AMY JOY DONUTS
CARIBOU COFFEE   DENIS KITCHEN AD AGENCY

Music Conducted, Orchestrated
    and Produced by . . . . . .MARK SUOZZO
Additional Conducting . . . . .JOSH ROSENBLUM

FEATURED MUSICIANS
Trumpet . . . . .DAVE DOUGLAS
Tenor Sax . . . . .BOB MALACH
Musical Saw . . . . .DALE STUCKENBRUCK
Violin Solos/Concertmaster .SANFORD ALLEN
Piano, Organ, Celeste . . . . .DEREK SMITH
Bass . . . . .JOHN BEAL
Drums . . . . .RONNIE ZITO

Music Recorded
    and Mixed by . . . . .TED SPENCER
Recorded at . . . . .CLINTON RECORDING STUDIOS
Additional Recording by . . . .BUTCH JONES at
                              BACK POCKET RECORDING
Mixed at . . . . .TRS RECORDING
Music Consultant . . . . . . .EVYEN KLEAN

Dave Douglas appears courtesy of RCA Victor Group